ANTH

CW00957283

2~~~

Hartlepool Writers Group

COPYRIGHT & DISCLAIMER

THE CONTRIBUTORS

Ange Dunn
Chris Robinson
Denise Sparrowhawk
Ethel Stirman
Irene Styles
J.K. Snowball
Joe Larkin
Kevin Horsley
Micheal Stevenson
Quentin Cope
T.H.

Publishing:Typesetting:Production

: Mecurian Books:

CONTENTS

THE HARTLEPOOL WRITERS GROUP (HWG)

Anthology 2020 showcases an eclectic mix of writing from participating members of the Hartlepool Writers Group (HWG). From Flash Fiction to Fantasy and Poetry to Romance the author/contributors to this fascinating 2020 Anthology are proud to present a series of work where hopefully every reader will find some particularly absorbing subject matter.

The need to write; the need to explore our minds and take ourselves to a different place on occasions is within all of us. The HWG is a collection of individuals who have a need to write; a need some would perhaps describe as a passion. By getting together once a month, and guided by HWG Facilitator Denise Sparrowhawk, members of the group are able to share their ideas, exercise some basic techniques and most importantly of all seek critique of their work from other members.

As more and more processed entertainment and thought divergence advertising bombards our modern lives, it is often difficult to consider starting the writing process. The pressures of caring for a young family perhaps leave little time for embarking on laying down a measured number of words; words that would be the beginnings of that elusive novel which is supposed to rest within the soul of all of us. Being a member of a writing group, such as the HWG, provides support, encouragement and most of all the confidence to grab any spare minute you can to get your thoughts down on paper.

So, we hope you will enjoy this varied anthology, provided without the use of hard and brutal editing. The poetic words, heartfelt emotions, spirited actions and possibly amusing storylines that lay between the pages of this book are those provided by the contributors as written, and we expect this to be the first in a series of annual productions.

~~~~~~

PART ONE
Fantasy

WILLIAM AND THE FORCES OF EVIL

BY
CHRIS ROBINSON

"What will you be doing this afternoon, William?" his mother asked as she took away his lunch plate: "Ginger and the others are all away, aren't they?"

William stared at the empty place where his plate had been. Both reminded him of the empty space his friends' family holiday plans had left him. He could never see the point of going away for holidays. The sea was a good enough thing to see once, and walking on sand was a change for once, but he didn't like swimming much, and in any case the waves kept getting in the way. What was more, there weren't any fish to see; probably because they had more sense than to go anywhere near humans splashing about. He had complained about this once and had been given a book on pond life and told to find some rock pools to study. He had searched for an hour and finally found one rock pool with nothing in it and nothing beside it except the end of an ice cream cornet and a starfish, both of which he could recognise anyway.

The starfish didn't move for a long time, and he began to wonder whether it was dead. He consulted the book, which said nothing on how to tell a dead starfish from a live one. Disappointed, he had returned, only to be asked where his book was. He went back to look for it, and found that he had dropped it into the pond. Its sodden condition was noticed when he rejoined his family, and the subject of pond life was not mentioned again. He was also expected to be interested in Punch and Judy shows, which he found rather dull, particularly compared to the vicar and his wife arguing in the garden of the vicarage.

This was a new show which William and his friends had discovered in the village, which, apart from being more varied and eventful, was also free. The vicarage garden was surrounded by a high hedge separating it from the wood where William and the outlaws often wandered. A discreet gap in the hedge had provided them with the full theatre to accompany the angry words which had drawn them there.

The vicar's wife had recently thrown a garden gnome at him, and he had tried to retaliate with a birdbath which he had managed to lift, but which had proved too heavy for him to do anything else with. Although he had failed, the size of the birdbath had impressed his invisible audience, since they knew that they would have been hard-pressed to raise it at all.

From the words the Outlaws had heard exchanged, it seemed the dispute concerned something to do with flower arrangements, which did not surprise them, since it was precisely the sort of thing they were used to adults arguing about.

William considered his lunch plate again. Ginger would be back in three days, and Douglas and Henry, the day after that. In the meantime, William felt that he could do no better with the afternoon than to return to the wood and the gap in the hedge and see whatever the vicarage garden might offer in the way of new entertainment. He would then be able to report further developments to his friends next day.

He thought of the vicar the last time he had seen him. Although he had not quite managed to lift the birdbath, William had been impressed by how near he had come.

"The vicar is very strong, isn't he, Mother?" he said as he finished.

Mrs Brown placed William's plate on the pile which the maid was about to take away.

"Vicars need to be strong, William." she replied, noting with pleasure William's interest in the human personality and spiritual matters: "Faith sometimes requires great strength."

"I mean, at lifting things up." William continued.

"He has to be able to lift people's spirits, William." his mother said.

"I was thinking about ..." William began, but decided not to mention the birdbath. He knew from past experience that it was something adults would refuse to believe, or fail to understand if they did. He might as well question the importance of flower arrangements.

"What were you thinking about, dear?"

"Just ideas." William explained, aware that this explanation, though explaining nothing, had always proved adequate in the past.

Mrs Brown smiled.

Faith is a very important thing, William." she said: "Faith can move mountains."

William thought of the birdbath again, but said nothing. Sensing that a reply was required, he merely murmured, "Yes, mother." Then, rather uneasy about the conversation developing any further, he got up from the table and announced,

"I think I'll go for a walk in the wood."

He strode quickly to the door, but was not able to escape as quickly as he wished since his older sister Ethel appeared in front of him, and stood framed in the doorway. She was dressed in a costume like one he had seen on a poster for a film called "Passion in Persia." It was a kind of long and flowing dress, with baggy trousers covering her legs. A light blue silk veil covered all of her face apart from her eyes, around which a lot of black had been applied.

"How do I look, mummy?" she said.

Mrs Brown looked up from the spoon she was drying.

"Very nice, dear. But don't you think that it's perhaps a little bold for the parish fête?"

"But, mummy, it is a fancy dress competition. One can hardly have a whole lot of people dressed as nuns."

"I suppose so, dear. I don't really know what people wear for fancy dress competitions."

"That's because it's the first they've had here. They've introduced a fancy dress competition in place of the flower arranging. People say the vicar's wife was behind it, because she was so furious that the vicar never awarded her flower arrangements the first prize."

William listened to this with only a fleeting interest since he was so eager to escape to the wood. Ethel seemed equally eager to remain in the doorway and prevent him.

"Can you let me through, please, Ethel?" he requested politely.

"Oh, all right." Ethel said, apparently not having noticed him in her eagerness to present herself to her mother. She moved a little, but not quite enough to allow William through, before asking him:

"How do you think I look, William?"

Aware that he would be denied passage until he had said something favourable, he muttered,

"All right." before moving forward a little.

Ethel remained where she was.

"Only all right?"

"No, very nice, Ethel. You remind me of a picture outside the cinema -"

Ethel smiled and moved away at once.

William quickly made his way to the hedge by the vicarage. He brushed through the gap which gave him a view of the garden. He was not much surprised to see the Vicar there, or to see the vicar alone.

He was however astonished to see him struggling with the birdbath again. His efforts to lift it were in vain. After several attempts he looked up and saw William. He waved him over.

"I wonder if you can help me with this birdbath, young man." he said. The tent hire people are coming very soon, and they have advised me that their new tent is bigger than the old one, and we won't be able to fit it in unless the bird bath is moved.

I thought that if I moved it myself it might save them some time, and it might also prevent it being damaged, since it's quite an old and valuable one. You know what removal men are like."

Together they tried to lift it, but it was too heavy even for both of them. The vicar took a handkerchief from his breast pocket and mopped his brow.

"Well, it was worth a try, anyway. Thank you, young man."

He pressed a shilling into William's hand.

"Were you enjoying your walk in the woods?"

"Yes, very much," William replied, hoping the vicar would not ask him any questions about different trees or flowers. He felt gratified when the Vicar did not.

"Nature is a great inspiration. All life is there, large and small, and, I suppose good and evil too. But among trees, one is reminded only of the good... However, I must go and wait for the tent. Goodbye, young man, and thank you once again." He returned to the vicarage.

William returned to the wood.

He had taken only a few steps when he found his way blocked by a monstrous creature. The same size and general shape as a tall human being, its head and body were formed more like those of a crocodile or lizard. Its skin was scaly, and a furious hatred seemed to burn in its eyes.

"I am the forces of evil!" it exclaimed.

William looked around him.

"If you're the forces of evil," he said: "why is there just one of you? You can't be singular and plural. Don't you know any French?"

"Only one of me," The monster hissed: "I am the one and only one! There is no other! There is only me, me, me! and I am everywhere!"

The monster's hiss turned into a murderous bellow.

"I   am   everywhere,   everywhere, everywhere!"

William looked at the forces of evil suspiciously.

"If you're everywhere, then what are you doing here?"

The monster pulled itself up to its full height.

"I am here, William Brown, because you are a magician!"

William looked the monster up and down.

"How do you know my name?"

The monster adopted a casual air.

"It is my business to know these things."

William snorted.

"Fat lot you know about magic. I'm not a magician. Wish I were. They gave me a magic set last year and took it away straight afterwards. There was this trick with a jug of water ..."

"But you are special!" The monster interrupted: "You are different from the rest. Haven't you ever suspected that you are different from the rest? Don't you know how you are different from the rest?"

William considered for a moment.

"I was the only one who didn't get wet."

"Fool!" the monster bellowed.

"That's what my brother said," William observed. "You remind me of him in some ways. Though he gave me half a crown the next day and said he was sorry for losing his temper at Christmas."

"I am no brother!" the monster bellowed: "I am here to destroy you and your magic! I have the power to destroy you."

William snorted contemptuously again.

"All right mister magic expert. You destroy me with ..."

William looked around him. Sunlight shone through the gap in the hedge.

"... with that birdbath. Bet you can't!"

The forces of evil hunched its back and uttered a cackle of nonsense. The birdbath shot up from its base and flew towards William. He dodged it in the nick of time, and it came to rest against a tree. The forces of evil crouched on the ground, hissing in frustration.

"You see?" it said: "I can move birdbaths."

"Yes," said William, "but I never said you couldn't. I bet you that you couldn't destroy me, and you didn't do that. You came quite near though."

The forces of evil crouched lower, making seething noises.

"I'll tell you what," said William, feeling rather sorry for the monster. "You did better than I thought. Show me what you can do with the birdbath once more. Move it back to where it was. And then try to destroy me again. You might come a bit closer. I'm no use at magic, but I'm very good at avoiding things. It's something I was born with. My father's always telling me how good I am at avoiding things. He says it's the one thing I can do. But you can have another try. Just move the birdbath back to where it was."

The forces of evil writhed, moaning.

"Go on, then," said William gently, patting the monster on the back.

"I can't!" the monster hissed.

"Of course you can," William assured him. "It's just what you did, only the other way round."

"No it isn't!" the monster croaked. "I am the forces of evil! I am the forces of evil!"

William considered this proposition in the light of his own.

"What difference does that make?" he said.

The monster rose to its full height.

"Can't you see?" The forces of evil screamed. "I can't move it back to an empty space! I can't move anything unless it's meant to destroy someone!"

William considered for a moment.

"Well, I'll tell you what. I'll go and stand where the birdbath is, I mean was. Then you can try to destroy me again. Then I'll come back to this end, and you can have one more try from that end like cricket. You've played cricket, haven't you?"

With a moan of intense pain, the monster clutched its stomach.

"Never mention cricket again!"

"Why not?" William asked.

"Never mention anything again! You have given me a pain which will last at least an hour. I will overcome it. I can move both of us into the future. I shall move both of us two hours forward in time and then I will destroy you!"

He cackled some more nonsense and the birdbath flew towards William. He evaded it just in time, and the birdbath thudded into the forces of evil's stomach, knocking him over and falling on top of him.

"I'm sorry," said William, "but you shouldn't have tried it then. I was between you and the birdbath, and when it didn't hit me it was bound to hit you. Are you all right?"

The monster uttered a howl of pain, followed by another, and then another as it struggled free.

"I am the forces of evil!" it bellowed, defiantly as it staggered to its feet.

As its cries died down, William heard noises from the vicarage garden. Time had indeed moved forward, and the fête was now in full swing.

"I think you should see a doctor," William said, looking at the forces of evil's midriff.

"I am the forces of evil!" the ogre bellowed again, hardly able to walk.

William took its paw.

"Just follow me," he said.

"I am the forces of evil!" protested the monster. "I am everywhere!"

"I know," said William, "but your stomach seems to be here, and there'll be a doctor somewhere behind the hedge."

"I am the forces of evil!" the monster croaked.

"Oh, hello, William!" Miss Bates, the village librarian smiled as they entered the garden: "I didn't know you were here. And how nice of you to bring a friend."

"I am the forces of evil!" the monster growled by way of introduction.

Miss Bates regarded the forces of evil admiringly.

"You do it so well!"

"I am the forces of evil!" the ogre insisted.

"A most appropriate choice." Miss Bates muttered approvingly. The ogre wilted.

"Is there a doctor or a nurse here?" William asked her.

"I think you'll find both in the tent." Miss Bates smiled, indicating the large marquee.

As the pair of them approached it, the monster continued to bellow, "I am the forces of evil!" Each time he did so, the people near him smiled. One or two applauded. One of the churchwardens appeared and patted him on the back, saying: "Thank you for making such a tremendous effort!"

Standing just inside the tent door he saw a woman in a nurse's uniform. Next to her was a man wearing a white coat and with a stethoscope around his neck.

"I am the forces of evil!" The monster screamed.

There were howls of appreciative laughter. Those who were sitting having tea at folding tables stood up and applauded. There were several cheers.

William was about to explain matters to the nurse, when he felt somebody's hand on his shoulder. It was the vicar, just outside the tent. William turned to him.

"How on earth did you manage it, young man?"

For a moment, William was at a loss what to say.

"Did you find some of your friends to move the birdbath? Somebody has just seen it at the edge of the wood. How thoughtful of you to move it completely out of the way. I have just inspected it, and it's completely undamaged! You must have been so careful. I cannot thank you enough. Do share this with those who helped you."

William felt a coin pressed into his hand, at once recognising the weight of a half-crown. The vicar at once turned towards the tent.

"But if you'll excuse me, I must go inside now and judge the fancy dress competition. I gather there's one most original entry..."

William stood outside the tent, fingering the two coins in his pocket, and considered his position. The precept 'easy come, easy go' was one with which he was very familiar. Several times already in his short life he had received unexpected gifts of money, only to suffer forfeiture and angry recrimination in the light of subsequent developments. The screams of "I am the forces of evil!" emanating from the church fête tent were not auspicious. Instinct told him to remove himself as far as possible at once. As he turned back towards the gap in the hedge, he glimpsed a veiled woman inside the tent, looking at him. He recognised Ethel. He also recognised the expression in her eyes.

"Could I have only one stewed prune, Mother?" William asked, trying not to sound too plaintive as he regarded the three on his plate with near-despair.

Plaintiveness had never worked with prunes before, and he had decided on a new strategy involving reasoned argument and a quiet decisiveness.

"I don't have much energy at the moment, and there isn't much energy in prunes. There's lots of energy in cream buns, and I'm sure one of those would do me much more good. And prunes are good for the compost heap. I think it's something to do with ..."

He searched his memories of what he had read in his father's gardening magazine for an appropriate word.

"Enriching the soil."

Mrs Brown regarded William's new approach with interest. She had not forgotten his encouraging signs of serious thought at lunchtime. Moreover, other mothers in the village had told her that persuading the young to eat prunes was always difficult.

"If you can eat two prunes, William, then you can have a cream bun, and one prune can go on the compost."

"Thank you, mother," William replied, adding by way of concession:

"Before I put it on the compost, I'll wash the custard off. Custard doesn't enrich the soil."

It occurred to Mrs Brown that custard on the compost heap might also give her husband ideas of an unfinished dessert, and she readily agreed.

"Did you see anything special in the wood, William?" she asked as she placed a cream bun on the cake stand and proceeded to pour the tea.

William finished his second prune in silence. He then attacked the cream bun with relish, answering after he had finished half of it.

"Only the forces of evil." he said: "Nothing special."

Mrs Brown continued to pour the tea. In one way, William's new interest in spiritual matters encouraged her, but seeing the forces of evil in the wood sounded rather like the beginnings of religious mania. Against that was William's idea that they weren't special. She had never heard of a religious maniac who didn't regard evil as special. She decided to adopt a cautious approach.

"Oh, really, dear. How interesting. Why don't you think the forces of evil are special?"

"Well, they're everywhere, aren't they?" William replied casually.

Mrs Brown smiled.

"Yes, of course, William. And I'm not surprised you are short of energy after encountering the forces of evil."

William shook his head.

"It's wasn't that, mother. It was moving a birdbath for the vicar."

Before Mrs Brown had time to express her approval, Ethel appeared. She was still in her oriental dress which looked slightly less exotic now that she was holding a large teddy-bear.

"Oh, hello, dear," Mrs Brown said, looking at the teddy-bear. "Did you win the competition?"

With his head down to avoid meeting Ethel's eyes, William hastened out, carrying his prune.

Ethel sighed and raised her eyes upwards briefly.

"I did in the end. There didn't seem to be much competition - a doctor, a nurse, a waitress, that sort of thing, when at the last minute this terrible creature appeared announcing himself as the forces of evil. The costume must have taken ages. And he must have practised the voice for weeks. But then, soon as the vicar told him he'd won first prize in the fancy dress contest, he had some sort of breakdown and they had to cart him off to the mental hospital. What made matters worse was that he'd sewn himself in. They were still trying to get his head off when they drove away. Anyway, after things had calmed down, they had the competition again, and I won this time. Though everyone agrees it'll be back to the flower arrangements next year."

Ethel paused for a moment.

"Oh, and Mummy -"

"Yes, dear," Mrs Brown replied. She had an idea what Ethel was going to say, and prepared herself accordingly.

"I rather think William had something to do with it."

"What makes you think that, dear?" Mrs Brown asked, as she remembered herself doing many times before.

Ethel hesitated;

"Well, mummy, I saw him there, and ..."

"Yes, dear?"

"He usually has something to do with it, doesn't he?"

Through the open door came the sound of a tap running. Then the door into the garden opened and shut.

Mr Brown looked up from the evening edition of the local paper.

"There's something here about that lunatic who appeared at the vicarage fête yesterday; forces of evil or something. It seems he escaped from the van on the way to the mental hospital and they haven't found him. The police are warning people he could be anywhere by now."

Mrs Brown put her knitting to one side for a moment.

"That's more or less what William said."

Mr Brown smiled.

"Exactly. Why the police are bothering to warn people I don't know. I can't see the forces of evil ever harming anyone. Not with boys like William around."

A SELL-SWORDS REGRET

BY
J.K.SNOWBALL

Ark 1: Morgan One-eye.

I do not in truth, know what drove me to write this. (Cabin fever and isolation, the fever I suppose; I don't know). We know monsters and evil men exist. What created such monsters and drive men to do the evils we are all vulnerable to do?

As children, we are told humans are tainted with both light and darkness. Not bad but not good either. Some are born into this world to do great deeds of good and others great and dreadful deeds of evil; a curse from the Ancient Elves for settling here and taking much of their home as our own. Some believe.

Personally, I believe every man has malice in his heart once you take away the things in his life he holds close to his heart. I myself I'm not a good man, I suppose like many of us I do what I do in this world to survive

My name is Morgan One-eye. I was a miner as a younger man, then a Man at Arms. Then, I was a sell-sword in service to Sir Edger Saltcliff, the Baron of Saltcliff, a coastal fishing and farming village on the Stormcoast and vassal to Queen Margot of the Kingdom of Draconia.

For five years I served that household. Originally I'm from Emerald Island, five miles off the Stormcoast. I was hired to train Sir Edger's militiamen, who at the time were a bunch of levy farmhands who didn't know their blades from their backsides. Alongside my regular duties of training militiamen, I would, from time to time, be asked to enforce tax collection and enforce the laws of the land for extra gold in my wage purse.

That made me a disliked figure to the common Salty's (a term for Saltcliff locals) over time. I didn't mind,I was well paid. (and for my love whisky I needed the money) To my shame, I was overzealous in extracting Coin from reluctant debtors. Roughing up tenants, threatening to destroy and take what little they had.

It came back to haunt me one day when a vengeful husband assailed me in The Blind Knight Inn, cracking a pot mug against my face with sharp shards cutting into my Left eye. (Thus my nickname) As blind and drunk as I was I beat him, almost to death, if my men hadn't restrained me in my bloody-blind rage. It wasn't the first time I would have beaten a man to death in a drunken blind rage.

Later I found out he claimed my constant harassing his family for unpaid taxes finished off his ailing wife. At the time I didn't care, I just did what I got paid to do. Now as I look back. I was a bully. I deserved what happened. Sometimes ... I still think I feel the blood of people I made suffer on my hands. I didn't notice it at the time, but the harsh taxations Sir

Edger imposed on his people to appease the Queen's annual tribute, the more desperate people became; turning to thievery and banditry, prostitution and contraband trafficking.

One morning, I was summoned to the Main Hall of the castle. When I entered, Sir Edger was sat upon his rotted wooden throne, surrounded by old banners and moth-eaten tapestries of the Household's glorious and noble history, now a distant memory. With his head cupped in his hands, his mood was depressed. He was an ill-tempered underhanded man. He ate too much, drank too much and was a stout man with a stouter temper, regularly taking his anger out on his servants.

The only person he would listen to at the time was his younger brother, Sir Douglas.

As much as Sir Edger loved his brother, he resented him too. As much as he might have wanted him to go off to war and never return, the fact was that he needed him; he needed his charm and reputation to keep his people passive and co-operative

On that morning Sir Edger explained to me he sent his brother to investigate a report of bandits and an outbreak of plague in the village of Crowfield the day before and hadn't been seen or heard from since. So he ordered me to go and find out what had happened to him.

~~~~~~

Ark 2: Dead Crops and Living Corpses

I set out from my quarters in the castle later that morning. I put on my chainmail hauberk, my long black leather-jerkin, fastened my arming sword to my belt, then collected the rest of my gear and necessary provisions. I fastened my late wife's' ring around my neck which I kept on a silver chain. I mounted my horse and then set off from green lush warm coastlands, to the colder forests and hills of the northern lands.

I set out alone. Many of the lads were engaged keeping peace and preventing civil unrest. (It didn't matter, I preferred to work alone). I took a sizeable flask of Dwarvenfire whisky to keep me warm and keep me company. At the time, I probably relied on whiskey's company too often to see me through the day.

I followed the Merchant's Road about twelve miles North to where reports of mysterious attacks and disappearances took place. They did not know what was happening. Reports claimed farmers were being attacked by bandits accompanied by creatures described as human, and yet not human led by a crimson-haired woman.

She was dressed in a black hooded tunic, coming out of the surrounding woods on the outskirts, taking food and supplies and even people, then disappearing as quickly as they came.

The village itself seemed rather uninviting, unsettling in fact. It was almost midday as I arrived towards Crowfield. The eye of the Sun had shut his gaze. A grey endless cloud filled the sky.

The fields surrounding the small village seemed neglected. The wheat crops seemed rotten and diseased, black and infested with legions of marauding flies eating at the corpses of the crops. The second I rode through I felt a sinister chill run down my spine, like icy fingers pressing against my skin. It was a malice breeze being carried by a mild wind which made the dark brown hairs on my arms erect with fear.

My horse shared my feeling, neighing and shaking its head and ears, as if being agitated by some unseen force. I took a swig of my flask. It made me a little warmer, and calmed my anxious nerves and racing heart and my thoughts a little numb.

The village paths were empty except for traces of blood sprinkled around here and there and signs of scuffles. There were no footprints to be tracked, nor bodies. I half expected to find farmers with horses and carts of wheat and children running around playing but not a soul to be heard or seen. The houses were small and shabby with straw roofs and fir-plank walls. Most appeared to be vandalized with some even burned to ashes.

I noticed all as I rode by. My horse's nerves failed after an angry rumble echoed through the clouds. With a loud neigh, it jerked upward, raised to stand on its back legs, throwing me off and escaping back the way we came. I tried to rally the damn beast, commanding it to stay. But, by the time I got to my feet, it was long gone. I was now stuck with no way back before the Sun sank behind the mountains and trees towards the east. For the time being I was very much alone

I ventured further into the village on foot, my sword arm, gripping the hilt of my blade. It was so quiet I could hear nothing but the steps of my black leather boots and my breathing. Then I heard faded screams and cries in the air. I looked into some of the homes for signs of what might have happened there (maybe some discarded family savings or valuables too.) Some of the houses looked already broken into with savagely broken doors, blood splats, torn rags of clothes, furniture turned over or broken. If anyone left in a hurry they took nothing with them. I then decided to investigate.

The King and Crow was my favourite drinking hole when I rarely past through there.

"On the plus side if the village is abandoned there will be more Ale and Whisky for me to get!" I said at the time.

I'm ashamed of it now. I went into a village with its inhabitants missing and possibility dead (or worse) and all I could think about was an abandoned Inn full of free whisky, mead and ale

It was a sight when I got there; windows smashed, the door splintered and scarred as if clawed by savage beasts. Bodies were scattered around the Inn; all dead it seemed. Swords and spears mark others with arrows sticking out of them with teeth and bite marks. Some were soldiers bearing The Baron's sigil. Others were peasants with pale complexions and balding heads displaying unusually long, sharp fingernails and black lidless eyes

I was about to go through the door when it burst open! A knight came stumbling out in front of me. His long leather surcoat and chainmail hauberk were all torn, bloody and marked with claws

"AWAY FOUL CREATURE!" cried out the injured man in pain.

I went to aid him. But, as I approached, another man burst out snarling and also covered in blood. He pounced on the man on the floor and began to claw at him like some savage beast. I grabbed him and threw him off, but, he got to his feet and turned his attention towards me.

His mouth and hands were dripping red. He himself seemed badly injured due to a festering gash on his neck. He appeared human, but his eyes were lidless, black as the night sky; his skin pale as parchment paper and missing patches of hair. He stood snarling at me for a moment, then, before I could blink and draw my sword, he pounced on me, showing long protruding dripping red fangs!

He was unusually strong for a scruffy skinny looking man at least in his late sixty's. Then rage took me. For a moment we scuffled, then, with all my strength I overpowered the feral man. He was on the dirt floor. I punched and I punched, out of both fear and desperate rage. I couldn't stop. In the end, his face was caved. Bits of his brain and blood painted the fist of my brown leather gloves with bits of his hair too, I think.

The man I saved was lying in the dirt path, injured and breathing heavily. I went to see what I could do for him when I took a better look at his torn surcoat. I noticed his sigil was a White Hippocampus on a sea of Aqua-blue. I recognised him, he was Sir Douglas.

To keep him stable I bandaged his right arm that had a fresh raw bleeding wound, which seemed to have cut down to the bone. I gave him a dose of an opiate vile I kept in my pack which I never really needed.

When I was normally in a fight or a skirmish I'd drink enough whisky beforehand to numb any sense of fear or pain. It would normally work me up into a fighting frenzy.

I waited a minute for him to calm and for the opiate to sink in, then I asked him what had happened to him and the people of Crowfield.

He explained briefly. I'll relay as best as I can remember.

"I set out yesterday morning with a band of thirty retainers, when we arrived here the village was in chaos, children attacking and eating their parents, houses bordered and ablaze!

The seemingly frail and elderly were overpowering and savagely biting strong young men and women. Along with dead crops and dark skies, I could not believe my eyes!" he said while coughing in pain.

"We fought the creatures at a great loss. Half my band perished in the initial attack. My remaining soldiers secured the village as best they could.

We re-grouped at the King and Crow to tend to the Injured and the sick. The surviving peasants warned us people who died from the sickness wouldn't stay dead for long and would re-animate and tear us apart! So I ordered the dead to be gathered and burned as soon as possible. Then a low chilling fog circled the village. A chill ran down my spine, an unsettling feeling came over me. For a moment or two, I was sure I saw a hooded figure staring at me from behind a thick veil of transparent grey far on in the fields. Then, out of the thick veil of grey, one of the villagers leapt on one of my men, tearing out his guts as easy as tearing into a cake. I cleaved off the peasants head with my sword, then we heard a collection of snarling noises coming from the fog.

"RETREAT, RETREAT, TO THE INN!" I ordered. Then my remaining soldiers, myself and the peasants fought our way back and barracked ourselves in the Inn. Overnight we fought off various attempts by them to breach our position. I pondered upon what could have done this, how we were going to get out of here. However, when I thought about the symptoms and actions of those creatures, I realized what they were. They were bloody vampires! But, I'd seen and fought vampires before but none this strong or as beastly-looking before, or in the numbers I had witnessed!

We held out till this morning when they managed to break in through the cellar. There were so many of them they overwhelmed us. It was a close quarter orgy of gore and violence! They flooded in that morning, biting snarling and clawing as we hewed, hacked and slashed at them!   Eventually, everyone fell. All the remaining peasants and all of my soldiers were gone, slaughtered! I was left against two. I sustained several injuries, I managed to strike down one before the other one forced me out of the Inn, as you arrived."

"Vampires!" I said out of disbelief. My priority was Sir Douglas' safety. I carried Sir Douglas as best as I could which wasn't easy. I'm a strong enough man but it's hard when you're carrying a man in full mail slipping in and out of conscious. The opiate sunk in by then and his speech was now quite babbled and slurred. He fell unconscious again in my arms and I had no choice but to take him back to Saltcliff.

Luckily, I managed to find one remaining Draconian Stallion in the stables. Before we left I couldn't help but see if I could grab a barrel or two from the King and Crow. Only ... when I saw the inside of the inn the image of horrifying slaughter and carnage, I can't even describe how sickening and horrifying it was.

I ran out immediately projecting a fountain of vomit onto the floor. I secured him with rope to the back so he wouldn't fall.

The Sun was now sinking behind the mountains to the north, maybe an hour before night time came.

We rode off back to Saltcliff. "So far so good!" I said out loud as we galloped down that desolate road. But, not before I set that Inn alight.

Ark 3: The Biter and the Fighter

It was well into the night when we arrived back at the castle. The chill in the air was settling in, painfully stiffening my muscles and bones. There were no stars, but the all seeing eye of the Moon was out in its full glory, lighting our way back in a pale dull light.

I kept my mind and eye on the road as best as I could (with the good eye anyway), then finally we saw the moonlight light up the castle and the torches and candlelight lighting up the village before it. I was calm then, we were back. I had done the job I was asked. I rode hard the last lap into the castle calling for guardsmen to help carry him to the Baron's personal fissions.

As far as I cared my job was done. I made sure The Black Swan was safe and would keep the peace once he'd recovered from his wounds. I was done for the day, I returned to my quarters to wash up and rest, ready to get started on training the men the next morning.

I reached my room and went to the small table with the silver bowl and slightly broken mirror I used to get washed. I took off the bloodstained gloves and started washing my hands. I examined the aged man stood before the mirror; my raven black hair with silver strands here and there in both my hair and beard. Looking at the painful scar and cloudy whiteness of my Left eye, I was barely able to recognise the man I'd seen in that mirror.

I would often close my eyes thinking of the image of my wife; two years I'd been without her by that point, two years since she died. My mind would flash from when we first met to the day I proposed and she said yes under our favourite oak tree. Our wedding day! Then, my mind turns to the day she was taken from me. I put my hands to my chest where her ring hung. My hand fell flat on my chest. To my shock, the ring nor the chain was there.

I went into a rage and a panic, my mind racing a thousand times to a thousand possibilities I paced back and forth wondering where it had gone, cursing loudly into the air. I then sank to the ground in tears. Then my mind flashed back to earlier that day when I fought the vampire attacking Sir Douglas. I then remembered, when he pounced on me he must have torn off the chain. I dreaded it but I knew I would have to go back to that village. I wasn't leaving it for scavengers to find! It was the only item I had left of my wife and a reminder of the man I once was.

Once more I collected my gear and mounted a horse from the castle stables. Before I left, one of the Baron's men called after me with a bag in his hand, and a note that read:

"Morgan, once again you've done my house a great service! For returning my brother safely take this bag of blasting powder sticks and five gold Griffins for your efforts.

"With Regards, your lord, Sir Edger."

I dismissed the soldier and inspected the bag. I picked out one of the blasting powder sticks and my mind flashed with memories of my boyhood. I remember my father taking those down with me and my young brother, to clear the rocks in the mines back home when I was a small boy. But, it was those things that weakened the structure of the mine and got my father and brother killed. My mind flashed to images of people full of blood and mud, carrying out the injured and calling for what help they could get. I gathered myself and rode off again under the pale moonlight.

I rode hard in the night back to that patch of cursed desolate land. I noticed a bright amber glow as I approached. As I reached the dead crop fields I tied my horse to a nearby tree hidden from view. I made my way quietly through the field towards the amber glow, faint shrill screams filling the air. It appeared to be coming from the village centre near the communal well. I then realized some of the houses had been set on fire.

I took cover behind a wooden fence, peeking over the top to notice the centre lit well enough by shadowy figures with torch lights. At least twelve had gathered in dark hooded-tunics, guarding one captive on his knees and hands tied clasped behind his head. One figure at the centre appeared taller and slender than the others. She pulled back her black hood; she appeared to be a woman, an Elven woman. Strange tattoo markings of a tree decorated her forehead, her long blood red hair with eyes and lips to match. She was beautiful in a seductive, deadly sort of way. She circled the man on his knees, brushing her long index finger under his chin. He was shaking and sweating. She appeared to speak to him softly, which seemed to ease the man's anxiety. Then, as quick as a flash of lighting she produced long fangs and buried them deep into the man's neck. Blood poured out like a crimson waterfall. His cries of agonizing pain filled the air and touched my soul with chilling dread.

She released him from her claw-like grip and used his rags to wipe the blood from her lips. She then began to speak to her followers in a language unfamiliar to my ears. I then noticed in the torchlight dangling from her neck was my wife's ring on its silver chain! I saw enough by then. I didn't have the patience to hear what her honeyed strange words had to say. I was frightened yes but, I was desperate to get that ring back!

I took another stiff drink from my flask, got out the blasting powder sticks, lit the fuses with a flint, then with an effort I threw the sizzling sticks of chaos and death. I saw them fly into the air then fall into the middle of the unsuspecting group, distracted by their parasitic leader. Then...BOOM!

The ground shook and rocked; a ball of flame, dust and earth engulfed the vampire and her acolytes! Some perished and were obliterated in the blast; some flew back by the blast wave! A light veil of smoke filled the scene, with the light smell of sulphur and scorched flesh

As if by instinct, I leapt over the fence, raised my sword and made my assault. I needed to act swiftly before they had time to recover from their daze. I could not see their leader; she was behind the veil of smoke and disturbed dust. One of them roared and charged at me; spear in hand, he lunged it at me but I was too quick for him! I grabbed that spear, pulled him towards me then ran my sword through his hooded face!

Another one sprang out from the shadows. That one was competent, I gave him that, sneaky too, he thrust with a short sword and a concealed dagger narrowly missing my chainmail hauberk. Our steel swords clashed and he swung high for my head. He would pay for that mistake! I went low and hewed his legs clean off! Another one ambushed me out of nowhere from my left side (my blind side), trying to bite at my neck. I struggled with that one over to the well. After a struggle I got the better of him, grabbed him and threw the sneaky biter into the blackness of that Well, his screams echoed as he went down into the darkness of that well until the echoing sound of his landing splash. Then she appeared.

She stood before me surrounded by a circle of her dead followers. Rage and a malice red flame I saw in her eyes under her black hood. An elven sabre, she gripped in her right hand. It was a standoff, a duel. We both stood opposing each other, studying each other, neither one daring to move. Then, like lighting she unleashed her attack! So swift she was I barely managed to react. (The whisky probably slowed my sharpness). Then clash! Our blades met in a deadly dance. For a minute or so, we clashed our blades, the sound of clambering steel ringing in the air.

I was stronger but she was swifter. We locked our swords for a moment. This was close. I could smell the death and blood breathing at me from her jaws; the strained but determined look in her face as she tried to win the deadlock, then, I felt a sharp pain shoot through my leg. I cried out in pain and retracted, dropping my sword, to discover the vampire whose legs I hewed off (but didn't finish off) got his teeth and claws into my ankle, giving his master time to recover. She kicked me away with such force, it felt like I was kicked by a horse. I flew and landed hard on the dirt ground, slightly winded and dazed, with my ankle in severe pain, and bleeding.

I attempted to get up but as quickly as I tried to raise myself, she put me back down hard. She was toying with me, wanting me to suffer. Savagely she pounced on me, her long fangs exposed. She was determined to make me one of her enthralled feral pets. It seemed the end for me.

While the vampire was trying to rip my throat out the legless follower of hers was crawling closer and closer towards me, armed with a sharp dagger and sharper teeth, wanting to save his master and finish his revenge.

Desperately I tried to keep the red-haired bloodsucker at bay. She was getting so close I could feel her breath against my skin. It smelled of rotten fish. I managed to grab a dagger on a body lying close to me. With a close strain and struggle, I managed to reach for that dagger and bury it into her skull. I remember the cracking sound of the bone and the stunning look in her blood-red eyes as the dagger passed sharply into her head.

I pushed her off and sprung to my feet grabbing a crossbow close to me. I used it to shoot at the legless one trying to escape after seeing the death of his master. I hit into his eye. He was not dead, lying twisting and turning in painful agony. I picked up my sword and ended his misery. The battle was over. I had won! I got what I went for, but at my own peril.

Once I was sure the Vampire and all her followers were dead. I limbered over to the one with my wife's ring and claimed it back. I started to investigate the bodies (or at least what was left of the bodies), mostly for trinkets, money, anything I could find useful really, not as they would be much use now it was more out of habit. To my shock, one of the bodies I found was the man who cut at my eye. In fact many of the bodies I found in that place were the bared, bloody and scared faces of people I helped drive further into poverty and despair.

The guilt I felt, knowing I had a hand in that. Turning people into slaves and soldiers for beings that are nothing more than parasites (soon I may be one of those parasites) feeding off the desperate, (and literally off their blood) recruiting them to their own selfish needs; lured to the prospect of false freedom and power.

An end to their hunger and an end to their suffering. A sense of safety and belonging. But, in reality, they're just victims. In the end, they just become food for their dark arts and appetites.

After I was done, I tore off a piece of the robe to stop my leg bleeding further (not that it mattered). I limbered back to the horse and rode off into the night. I didn't know where I was going but I couldn't return to Saltcliff.

My leg was in such pain it felt like it was burning and being stabbed repeatedly with sharp, salted blades. My mind raced considering what I might become and what I should do. I couldn't think clearly, all I did was ride off until I could think of something.

Ark 4: The Dawn

After some wandering in an unfamiliar country I discovered a small abandoned fisherman's shack by a lake. My vision began to flare and I grew weaker by the hour. I couldn't escape what I knew was clear by then, so with what little time I felt remained to me, I decided to write this down.

The confessions of a dying man (or a cursed one) you might say. I reflect on the decisions I have made in my life leading up to this; the people I loved and cared about; the people I've lost and the people I've wronged and harmed. I have many regrets, but nothing I can do about it now, except maybe just cling to the few happy memories I have till this sickness takes me or I decide to end this misery. Maybe I deserve it, who knows?

The wound on my leg turns blacker and a deep burning pain intensifies by the hour. Fever has set in and my hands tremble, my head dripping with sweat. Not long now I think. Time is very short. I have a decision to make. To linger on in the shadows like a vampire; hunt those who made me this way or die my way and reunite with my wife.I know what I have to do.

The Dawn will rise over the mountains soon. I'll walk over to the lake, her ring in my hand my sword in the other. I'll sit there a while in the cold dark, pondering my fate in my ever ailing state, waiting for the sun to rise and feel its warmth against my face one last time; watch as the light dances on the rippling water. I must go soon, I have a choice to make ... to end my life or accept my un-dead fate.

~~~~~~

My First Prey

This is a diary extract found among the bodies, littering Crowfield that morning after the skirmish that took place in the late hours of the night. It was discovered by Sir Douglas and his retinue when they arrived that morning; discovered in a pool of blood by a discarded sabre. Most of the writing was too soaked in blood to read except for this small piece.

20th Seedling of Spring1401.

"I didn't want to do it" I thought to myself. But, I had to. To survive I would need to drink, to drink the blood of the living. There was no going back now. My lover told me I had to get strong or I'd end up like the "Rotters" we had infested the small village of Crowfield with. Infecting their crops with our blood

I remember before I left for my first feasting he placed his kind hands on my shoulders and said "Go forth now my sweet, I have plans for you when you return, in this ever-changing immortal game."

He then kissed me on my forehead and I went forth to do his bidding. I appeared confident but I was actually rather hesitant and afraid.

At the time I wondered if I could do it? Would I hesitate? Is my half-life worth the life of an innocent? I would soon find out if I had what it takes.

I had never killed anything living before (or eaten it raw either). Would my victim be a stranger or a stricken family member or dear friend I left behind, to be with my lover.

My first prey was traumatizing, to say the least, short, awkward, but, also intoxicatingly exhilarating. I came across a peasant, who was old and grey. He appeared to have not bathed for days which made him less appealing to be my first prey.

His odour of local Dwarvenfire whisky was overpowering my new heightened senses. I certainly hoped he would not taste as bad as he smelled. I remembered him; his name was Bill the village drunk

I watched from the shadows of the trees and shrubs, on the right side of the old Merchant's Road. The old man was drunk and merely singing loudly staggering with glee. (Probably going home after a few whiskies down at the King and Crow, no doubt). I waited to strike before it was too late, before the night grew too old. I almost felt sorrow for old Bill, whose life I was about to take. I would make my slaying quick, so he would not suffer much pain, or suffer my un-dead fate.

I then thought "What if Bill himself was already diseased? What if I get tainted from the old man's blood?"

I then realized I am disease. I am a plague. I am death. I am a vampire! Then as if by instinct, I sprang forth from the shadows of the trees and shrubs, like a predatory wolf assailing an ailing old mutt.

I remember the frozen look of terror in his old grey eyes as I grasped my hands around his arms and buried my fangs into his neck. I remember the crunching sound of my teeth scratching on his collar bone and the squishing sound as his fresh, warm blood flowed from his throat. His pain-induced screams echoed up into the cold night air. I was animalistic; I could not control the need, the lust for a living man's blood. I wrestled him to the ground. He could do little to resist, except scream and cry in pain as I sank my fangs deeper into flesh and bone.

It was over. He was dead. I withdrew my fangs that were now dripping crimson-red. I was now filled with a strange exhilaration that I only ever experienced after sex. I looked at my hands that were also painted red. Guilt filled my head. After all in my former life, he was my mother and father's dearest friend. I didn't want to slay him, but it had to be done. Maybe not him, but I was going to need to drink blood sooner or later. Or in Bills case a slow painful death of the disease we spread or in his case "The Black Liver".

To keep me sane I told myself I gave him mercy. It was quick. This was not my choice. This is my fate, to survive by feasting on those who walk in the day. If not, I would decay; lose my new found eternal beauty, lose my hair, develop paler skin and lidless black eyes, lose my mind and become a Rotter; one of my fellows who refuse to drink and become feral beastly monsters in exchange.

I stood there for a moment looking into the eye of the Moon. I heard an indistinct collection of voices in the air and footsteps hurrying down the road. The villagers and militiamen were coming, accompanied by their bloodthirsty dogs (that stupid Sir Douglas too I should think). I knew then I had to go. I left him on the road for the villagers to find or as leftovers for the wolves and crows.

I ran as fast as I could, under the shadows of the night; they will never catch me. I reached our Coven's den in the old abandoned coal mines with my lover and the rest of my friends. Here I remain until nightfall, to go hunting again. When I stood before him upon my return, he placed his hands upon my shoulders "It is now the time my Crimson-haired Shadowblade."

I knew then our time was close. I did as he asked; he could trust me to do his bidding. Crowfield was the start. We plan to spread our blood into the remote villages and towns, enthralling them to our cause. We wouldn't need to hide much longer. We would soon have an army. Soon, we would have a kingdom of our own.

TALE OF A FALLEN HERO

BY
MICHEAL STEVENSON

Imagine for a moment you are standing in an imposing cathedral like throne room, in the presence of a King with Lords and Knights surrounding him, when suddenly, he rises and calls for your execution. Yeah, not something you'd expect when you've not long saved the King and his whole country from disaster is it?

I should have noticed it. Something unsettled me the moment I set foot in the place. I felt a malevolent surrounding presence with the attendant Royal guards looking visibly tense. They remained steadfast draped in impressive silver armour, their eyes turned staring daggers in my direction. One simple word came to me at that moment; Hatred. I had been caught unawares to say the least when the guards all drew their blades simultaneously, their faces masked by sneers from under their polished plated helms.

You must be wondering what happened? What did I do to deserve this? To answer that, I must go back to the beginning; to the day they summoned me to this place.

My name is Zain Fairman, twenty-eight years old, and just like in those other fantasy tales, I have been summoned to another world. I would describe myself as your average guy in both stature and build with short jet-black hair. Born to a wealthy family, I had nothing refused to me as a child. I knew no real strife. But my early and previously happy life means nothing now; it simply does not matter.

~~~~~~

It felt as if I was in water, floating in a sea of nothingness. I heard strange voices all round me, and then I hit the cold hard ground. That was the moment I was to be taken from my existing life; the moment when I was to be summoned to another world.

I looked around the small room, my eyes feeling heavy, body difficult to move with any ease and my muscles noticeably weak. I was in the middle of a glowing purple circle surrounded by people in black robes, all chanting in a strange language; an alien noise to me, words that seemed impossible for humans to speak. Everything was about to go black once again.

I awoke once more in an unfamiliar bed. My own clothes were gone, leaving a set of grey garments stacked on a table near to me. Getting dressed came with a challenge I wasn't expecting. Not that it was difficult, but the style of the clothes appeared to be of a simple fifth century design, the trousers being three times the size of my waist and therefore wrapped around me with string to stop them falling.

"Is someone playing a joke on me?" I asked myself.

As I pulled the loose top over my head, for a moment, I thought a friend would jump out laughing at me with phone in hand recording my confused reaction. It sounds like something my old friends would do, except they never left me naked.

It didn't take long for someone to check up on me. She entered the room, her kind purple eyes looking directly at me. She wore a fantasy-like silky robe over a delicately detailed white dress. I felt myself becoming nervous, caught off guard by her beauty. She was saying something in the same strange tongue as the people in the black robes. My heart started racing, a strange pressure building up in the back of my head. However, after about a minute, her words changed. Little by little, they became familiar.

"Can you understand me now?"

She spoke with a kind, even, educated tone and in English.

"Yes," I replied nervously. It felt like my chest was about to collapse in on me; my heart refused to slow down.

"What a relief. My arcane skills are not what they used to be. Please, take a seat," she directed me to sit on my bed. "What you are feeling is a consequence of my magic, it'll pass shortly. Please take deep breaths and try to calm your racing heart."

I did what she said, taking huge deep breaths, although it didn't really help much. Despite my upbringing; no, maybe because of my upbringing, I've always had an issue with speaking to woman I found attractive. She spoke once more.

"My name is Alice Sefare. I am a priestess of the Holy Trinity."

"Zain Fairman. Nice... to meet you..." I stumbled over my words, feeling overwhelmed when I realised she had mentioned magic.

"It is a pleasure to meet you Sir Zain."

I felt like my head was going to explode. I knew, from the moment she sat down next to me, brushing her long golden hair back behind her head, I had become quite flushed. A slight panic had come over me.

"However, I'm afraid I am not an available suitor for you."

I found it odd she would say that; we had only just met and already she's rejecting me; I hadn't flirted with her or anything like that, did I?

We sat there in awkward silence for a moment as my heart finally began to slow.

She told me I had been summoned to be a noble hero, to save their world from a monstrous demon that had been terrorising them and I was the only one who could stop it... talk about cliché.

She told me of the world they called their own. I was in the Vica Kingdom, a Human Kingdom that rivalled most others in the land. From what I could gather, I had arrived in a fantasy world at a similar development level to medieval Britain, around the fifth or sixth century, with the added inclusion of Elves and Dwarfs, Beastmen and Lizardmen and other such fantasy beings. Then she told me about magic and the gods. I must admit I struggled with that last part. Their gods lived among them, secluded in remote locations around their world. Some were good while others were not. As a priestess, she worshipped the human gods of Light and Earth, but when she spoke their names her words became muddled, distorted, sounding strange and unearthly.

After several clumsy attempts to question her and with the added difficulty of hiding my obvious attraction, she took me to see the King of the land.

I was overwhelmed by the commanding structure as we walked through the castle. It was massive in scope, highly detailed and decorated with a vibrant mix of colours. I had seen castles in England, but they were nothing like this. My professor would have had a field day exploring this magnificent place.

The King sat slightly uneasily on his throne in the large throne room surrounded by armoured royal guards, standing silent and firm with obvious purpose. The lords of the court sat expectantly in rows of three to either side of the throne.

King Earl Bardol most definitely looked the part, resting upon his elevated throne at the end of the cathedral like hall; a gold crown sitting perfectly on his head and wearing clothing befitting a ruler; reds and blues with amazingly delicate gold detail.

He didn't speak directly, letting his advisers speak for him as he looked down on me. They promised a just reward for saving the Kingdom from doom and to help me, they offered a choice of impressive looking mythical armour and weapons. But before I could take any, the King ordered I provide a suitable demonstration of my abilities.

I was afraid at first. I've only ever practised sparring with a sword and shield amongst my college classmates, however my skills were not to be taken lightly as I was close to obtaining my master's degree and planning to open my own class in swordsmanship. It felt different holding a sword again and this particular one felt very light.

A guard stepped forward, volunteering to spar with me; a disconcerting, twisted looking grin revealed from beneath his helmet. And so we began, our swords meeting in the air. I intended to let his blade pass, a deflection so I could disarm him. However, I overextended, he was thrown back from the impact, his blade flying from his hand as he hit the ground hard, holding his arm in pain. I had broken his hand, leaving me frozen in place, terrified over what had just happened.

"You are indeed the hero of legend," The King exclaimed delightedly.

That was the first time I heard his booming voice, you'd have no issues knowing when he spoke. He seemed very pleased. His advisers explained to me what had just happened. When I was initially summoned, my body had been infused with magic making me stronger and faster. Adding that effect to my existing skills had made me feel near to unstoppable. I had no reason to suspect anything unusual, so I decided to accept the quest. To prove I was serious, I knelt down to show proper respect in front of a King, vowing to kill the demon threatening their kingdom. I was soon ready to be on my way. It was time to save the world and become a fantasy-like hero, or so I thought.

~~~~~~

I knew too little of the world I was now in; I needed to fix that. Before I left, Alice gave me a brief rundown of the culture and customs. As I suspected, technology-wise the kingdom lived in a time of development similar to the fifth century. Fashion looked to be quite varied, almost as if it came out of a fantasy book, and the use of magic made technological advancements unnecessary, they use magic for pretty much everything. Culture, however, was substantially different to what I expected in terms of my own historical studies. I had expected woman to be treated quite badly for example, but in reality, they held substantial power and mostly controlled the noble houses. The last bit of advice Alice gave me before I had to leave was about relationships. Women were positively in charge of a relationship, in terms of when it is to begin, when and if it advances and when it eventually ends. It wasn't necessarily related to law but seen more as custom. If a woman chooses to be with a particular man, they usually get their way.

"So what you're getting at is, women chase men here and not the other way round?" I asked. She nodded in agreement.

She warned me about some types of women who liked to take advantage of this useful arrangement and recommended I should think carefully about accepting any invitations I may receive. This was defiantly strange for me to hear, but I could tell she was only concerned for me, I thanked her for the advice. Now it made sense why she rejected me when we first met.

The conversation with Alice had increased my general level of anticipation. As a history buff with a love of the medieval period I looked forward to the possibility of exploring the city and other areas surrounding the castle. However, my quest could not be kept waiting and time was now of the essence.

Three adventurers were assigned to me, to guide and help me. We quickly exited the city at the break of dawn with our prearranged supplies. I didn't see a single soul as we started our journey out of the city.

Axel Barflow appeared to be the leader of the small band of travelling companions. He showed himself as being arrogant but confident, barking orders left and right no matter how foolish they appeared to be. I didn't like him much; I got the impression of rudeness and disinterest from him; I guess I wasn't accustomed to the social norms of this world yet, although I couldn't fault his skill with a sword. He was a tall, strong framed individual with simply styled short brown hair and never seen without his well-used set of old iron-like plate armour that still shined in the sun.

Elias Seacrest, the second of what I assumed was the male in the group, was a strange one. He held an unsettling shifty look in his eye and possessed a set of unusually sticky fingers. I told myself to be sure to keep a close eye on my money and other valuables when he was around. He was, to all who knew him, simply a tiny little bastard who loved to practise and play around with knives. I definitely didn't trust him... or like him. He could also not be parted from a tattered brown cloak which he wore constantly in an effort to partially hide his face. He never spoke a word when I was around.

Finally, there was Alaya Godwing. I found her quite cute at first with glistening green eyes and a tempting body. She acted like a little child in most situations despite being a grown adult. She always had a bow on her but I had never seen he use it. Instead, she would regularly practise launching small rocks using a slingshot. I couldn't doubt her skill with it and she always looked to hit her mark. She possessed magnificent tresses of long jet-black hair framing a slim, athletic figure being quite short compared to the rest of us. If I had been a few years younger, I might have fallen for her particular look and regularly revealing outfits. At our very first meeting I found her annoying and therefore ended up not liking her all that much. However, a strange, possibly disturbing feeling enveloped me every time I looked at her.

We were heading to a dungeon complex called 'The Cursed Caverns'. According to Axel, the Dwarfs had built a stronghold deep inside a mountain many generations ago. To get to it, we would have to navigate a series of underground caverns built originally for the Human Kingdom. Something had happened in the past; something to do with the misuse of magic; something that caused the Humans to abandon the place. 'The Cursed Caverns' had been named as such by the locals because of the monsters who moved in later. Conversely, I discovered later that the caverns themselves weren't actually cursed.

I found our voyage to the caverns quite a strange affair. There were no villages or towns on the way. We simply followed a dirt road on the back of a horseless carriage pulled by magic forces. It took about a week of travel and I got to know Axel and Alaya more during the journey while Elias remained quiet throughout with rarely a word spoken. During this time the first impressions of my travelling companions were up for review. Axel had become quite competent as a leader, although still a little arrogant. I wouldn't say we were due to become friends on a journey regularly spoilt by his constantly irritating talk about how many women he'd been with and how Alaya had regularly refused to sleep with him. To be honest, I found him generally a little creepy. Alaya on the other hand still aroused that strange, uncomfortable feeling in me every time I looked at her. Something felt very out of the ordinary about her, something I couldn't really explain. By the third day into our journey she had begun to act much more maturely and eventually, as the days passed, she developed distinct signs of warmth toward me. On the last night, the night before we reached the caverns, she sneaked into my tent. She said she wanted to have 'fun' before the big day. Her definition of fun was sex with no strings attached. That was the first time I saw her without that uneasy feeling, I'm a weak man, we had 'fun' throughout the night, leaving me with the uncomfortable impression that this was what Alice had warned me off, I kind of felt used, but for some strange reason I didn't mind at all, it was a good night, very... different to what I'm used to with my sexual partners for sure.

~~~~~~

The entrance to the dungeon gave off a dark and ominous air. A substantial stone archway marked the darkness of the passage we would be going into. The demon claimed this dungeon as its base and I'll admit, initially I was quite hesitant.

"Be careful, there is strange magic here. It'll take us a while to get through it."

The magic Axel was talking about had been made to deter trespasses from entering the stronghold, creating unexpected twists and turns through the caverns instead of a simply straight path leading into the labyrinth. The only way forward was to just walk through it. If the magic wasn't present, Axel said it would only take a few minutes to pass through.

After several hours of exploring the winding tunnels and stone carved passages, and with our only light being a flaming torch that somehow never went out, we ended up finding nothing. There appeared to be no rooms. But there were many splitting paths that seemed to loop back on themselves. We stopped for a break. Axel and Elias scouted on ahead while Alaya stayed with me, preparing food for everyone.

I don't know if it was the necessary spell she had cast for the provision of light or just the light itself contrasting with the blackness of the shadows, but Alaya appeared different to me now as she sat there, busy preparing food. The strange feeling I previously had about her had disappeared.

I stared at her, near mesmerised as I followed every detail of her actions like some schoolboy daydreaming about his first crush. Maybe I had her all wrong. Her expression, while focusing on her tasks, and the way she acted at that very moment prompted an overwhelming attraction for her that that has been building within me since the night before.

She noticed my thoughtful gaze and started coming on to me.

She moved closer, offering some of the food she'd hastily prepared, studying me with the kind of look that shouts desire.

She whispered in my ear things I could scarcely believe, never thought I'd be in the company of someone who could be that lewd. It was an uncomfortable, but unavoidable turn on.

Fortunately, at that very moment the others came back. I was confused and didn't know what to do. I had been frozen where I sat, unable to speak or react.

It was a strange if not disturbing moment for me. I like my women a little more on the mature side and classy, very much like Alice. No, that isn't fair is it. I am attracted to confident women who know what they want and know how to get it. Alaya had that particular attribute in spades. I never thought I'd be attracted to someone like her, but I am. I've only lain with women I've been romantically involved with, Alaya was barely a friend at this point, it did get me thinking however, maybe we could enjoy some form of romance, now more than ever. I now found myself in completely unexplored emotional territory. I looked to Axel and Elias for their fortuitous return with some form of gratitude none the less. However, looking at them, something felt off, maybe even wrong with them, I felt that strange feeling emanating from Elias for some reason, it was the same feeling I had previously felt from Alaya when I first met her, something was wrong, I could feel it in my gut.

~~~~~~

We continued onward, deeper into the caverns. It felt like hours finding nothing in the seemingly unending tunnel until we came across the entrance to a large cavern. Alaya and Elias went on ahead of us. While Axel and I took a moment's breather, I wasn't used to all this moving around, a loud noise that echoed around the cavern disturbed us. Alaya had unfortunately triggered a trap; it took her down in one go, the result of perhaps a small explosion. She was alive but knocked to the floor and obviously hurt.

Monsters came streaming out of nowhere, yelling and screeching furiously. Axel and Elias ran into them, fighting them off as best they could while I stayed with Alaya, hoping to protect her from the monsters aiming to finish her. They moved like we did and even displayed some notable skill with the swords they carried. This was to be my first life or death battle. I was afraid, but I was also stronger, faster and more skilled than they were so didn't have need for the small shield on my back. I easily killed all who challenged me in single swings of my sharp red steel sword. It was a jarring moment realising I had killed monsters displaying signs of obvious intelligence and physical coordination. Although I doubted my actions, I knew what I had to do, telling myself they were evil and had to be stopped, right?

Once the Monsters saw how out-matched they were, they ran, inhuman ugly screams of panic and fear echoing as they left their dead and dying behind. We had won but now my attention had to return straight back to Alaya. She had a wooden shard sticking from her leg as a result of being caught in the trap, her clothes singed and torn from the heat of the explosion. I panicked, not really knowing what to do.

She reached down, pulling the shard out of her leg, something which didn't help matters. She was lucky it wasn't deep and hadn't cut an artery. I sighed with relief as Elias bandaged her up. In that particular moment I realised how much I truly cared for her, more than I should perhaps.

"Can you walk?" Axel asked her.

"Yeah, it's not that bad."

I considered retreating back outside, but she shot me down fast. She wanted to continue on and so did Axel and Elias. I felt defeated, like maybe I was being too cautious. I looked down at Alaya, thankful she was okay, but then it struck me again; that strange feeling impressing itself on my mind and definitely coming from her now. The battle had shaken me up, maybe I was imagining it. I was confident we could win whatever battles lay ahead. We would return as heroes; heroes who had saved the world. Alaya also appeared to have been really shaken up, although she would never admit it. She now moved with a limp and used my arm for close support, hugging perhaps a little too close for comfort. Fortunately, we encountered no further resistance.

Finally making it through the caverns it felt like days had passed but I'm sure it was only a few hours. The magic in this world is impossible for me to understand. I guess that's why they call it magic? Making the impossible... possible! The tunnel had by now opened up into a massive cave big enough to fit a small village and lit by a glowing roof of blue; an amazing magical sight to behold. A massive stone fort-like structure stood at the far end of the void, carved out of the solid rock and just about what you'd expect from Dwarfen architecture identified by its thick chiselled pillars and impressively deep walls.

Alaya suddenly fainted, collapsing onto me. I should have known something was wrong, she'd been out of breath and leaning on me more than usual. We made a small camp, away from direct view of the fort.

I tended to Alaya's bandages, concerned her cuts had possibly become infected, but the wounds appeared clean and healing. I hoped letting her rest up would help, however she wasn't getting better, in fact she was weakening fast. When she awoke, she began experiencing pain all over her body.

"Looks like poison," said Axel solemnly, "these creatures use poison on the strong and foolish, they even coat their swords in it. It's deadly and made to make the victim suffer terribly."

I wanted to punch Axel for not telling me this sooner, purposely holding back vital information like this.

"Do we have a cure?"

My question was met with an ominous silence. It was as if my entire world had just fallen apart. I couldn't accept it, I wouldn't accept it! Even if I didn't feel these dammed emotions for her, I couldn't just let a comrade die like this. I wanted to go back, take Alaya back to the city we came from and find a cure for her. However, it was already too late. She was going to die and there was nothing I could do to stop it. "Please...?" she begged, taking my arm, stopping me from arguing with Axel on what we should do, "please, kill me...!"

I froze with dread and on the verge of tears. She asked me to put an end to her pain; to take her dagger and end her life. She didn't want to die as a result of the poison. It would be a fate worse than death itself, to suffer through it all.

We hugged, whispering in my ear as she handed me her dagger, readying herself for the end. She held my hand as I prepared myself, her grip becoming weaker. She told me she loved me, and she wouldn't want anyone else to do what she had asked, the remaining light in glistening eyes fading to nothing as I finally took her life.

"Thank you…" she offered faintly, her departing words carried on one final dying breath.

I had killed her, and now her blood would be forever on my hands.

Axel and Elias gave me time alone. I needed to clear my head. She told me before she died to continue on; kill the monsters trying to kill her people. She believed I could do it. It devastated me; to witness her death right in front of me; to take her life. I crumbled down into tears.

An uncontrollable rage built up within me. I vowed to take vengeance for her death and nothing else mattered now.

It was soon time. I took Alaya's dagger, securing it to my belt, and we made our way up to the large wooden doors of the stronghold.

~~~~~~

We entered the fort. I stayed up front this time. I wasn't about to let the others put themselves at unneeded risk. Also, I was itching for a fight.

For the first time, I slid the small round shield from my back and attached it to my arm. I didn't care if I needed it or not; I wasn't about to let them poison me.

My thoughts lingered on Alaya and her passing. I was still in shock; still enraged. I wanted to kill them all for what had happened. Inside the fortress all appeared well lit and bright. There were few dark corners or shaded spots where enemies could hide in ambush. We fought through a few small groups of guards, killing them with ease and ruthless efficiency, entering a large throne room at the centre of the fort. There it was, standing in the middle of a group of repulsive looking minions.

My target had to be the monstrous demon. It looked quite disgusting with constantly morphing features and horns protruding out of its head.

"That's it, the demon we've come to kill," declared Axel: "The Demon Lord..."

I didn't question it. Perhaps I should have. All I heard was this was my target, the one upon which I must take vengeance for Alaya's death. It grunted and growled at its attendant minions, holding out a restraining hand. It wanted to fight me one on one. It lifted up a sword, the action of a knight before taking up honourable combat. I thought it was mocking me, but respecting swordsmanship rules, I did the same back.

"It's mine! Keep out of this event ... both of you," I said to Axel and Elias, "keep an eye on the minions, if they attack ... kill them all."

It was time; the final battle ... the boss fight!

My anger boiled over as I watched the demon's movements.

"A purely defensive stance is it?"

I had tunnel vision, but instinct had kicked in, telling me to be careful. I couldn't just rush in like I had done with the others. It continued to snarl at me as if it was trying to communicate. Neither of us wanted to attack first; I had no idea how powerful it was; how skilled it possibly could be. None of its minions truly posed a threat; even a novice who has never carried a sword could have bested them with the power boost I had. But this one was different and something was telling me he must be considered dangerous, even for someone like me.

I'd had enough of waiting; I rushed in, sword pointing at him in a thrust. He deflected my attack easily leaving barley enough time for me to raise my shield to defend against his counter. It had become intense as we backed away from each other. He was no doubt as strong as I and just as fast. The only way I could win would be to out-skill him. We were both hesitant to engage, with each violent clash comprising blocks and deflections. Neither had an obvious advantage and one mistake could spell our doom. It kept on trying to talk to me in strange growling murmurs.

"Don't listen to it! It's trying to overtake your mind!" Axel yelled out.

That's when all hell broke loose as the other minions attacked Axel and Elias. They left me alone with their leader; my target. It was time to get serious.

The battle was hard fought. It reminded me of training in a way. No one could normally beat me using mediaeval styles of combat but I kept on losing ground, taking light blows to my deflecting shield with my sword being parried by the Demon. Finally, I knew I had to make my move, sliding off my shield and throwing it at the creature, like a comic superhero.

It caught the Demon Lord completely off guard and in that moment I ran full speed at it, taking my sword and sliding it forcefully into its gut. It felt like I had run into a brick wall. We both hit the ground hard with a thump as I gained the advantage, managing to get on top of the slippery creature. I took Alaya's dagger and stabbed the near defeated demon in the heart. It issued a mighty scream of rage and pain... and then it was all over.

Everything had happened in a flash; I had won. I killed the Demon Lord. I stared at its warped and lifeless face, my anger, my fear and my pain remaining. This triumph had bought me no satisfaction or peace.

Although it was a hard-fought battle, I realised how easy it all had truly been. We had taken the fortress single-handed with the demon's minions showing themselves as weak and untrained. The demon himself had skill and could match me in most circumstances but an army of professionals could have done the job just as well. I was sure of it. Why then... why couldn't the King just send his troops to deal with this? Why go through all the trouble in summoning me?

These uncomfortable thoughts quickly vanished from my mind as the emotional pain and grief returned. Alaya was dead, and it was my fault.

I cut off the demon's head and placed it in a bag. We were done. It was time to return to the King. Axel and Elias had dealt with the minions and they weren't even out of breath.

We returned to collect Alaya's body, but Axel stopped me.

"Leave her be!"

I wanted to carry her home but, he was insistent we leave her.

"We can't just leave her here Axel."

I convinced him to give her a proper burial at least, even if it was an unmarked grave just outside the caverns. I hated every moment of it, as if on cue, like some sort of bad cliché, it started raining, at least the weather matched my mood.

As we travelled back to the Kingdom, Axel and Elias seemed distant. I gained the impression that Alaya's death had meant little to them. They both acted as they normally did showing little signs of sorrow or concern. Elias continued to hide his face, never speaking, while Axel carried on verbalising annoyingly about his… 'conquests'.

On the journey back, neither would show any sign of change in their attitudes. I was too engulfed in my grief to truly question the situation. I just wanted to get everything over and done with. I was such a fool. Nearing the city on the last morning, I noticed Elias wasn't feeling well. Axel said he was sick and wouldn't be joining us for breakfast. I didn't think much of it being more concerned about the possibilities of him making me sick too, although he was acting a little strangely around me, even for him. At one point, I caught him staring at me, for a moment, I thought I saw the glimmer of feminine green eyes, the same as Alaya's. When I took a second take, he'd quickly turned away.

"Has to be my imagination," I told myself.

~~~~~~

We had returned to the Kingdom and the moment I stepped into the royal court I realised something was not right. The cold, detached stares of the royal guards should have been a good enough hint. I knelt offering respect to the King. I told him what had happened on our journey, how we had killed the demon and lost Alaya. Axel proudly presented the severed head of the Demon Lord to the King. Then, well, you know what happened next. The King stood and ordered my execution!

That was the last thing I remember before beginning to re-live those same events over and over again. The facts were I had been summoned to another world and asked to kill a demon. Part of that journey would be the unfortunate death of Alaya, the killing of the Demon Lord and my return to face the King. It felt as if I was watching rerun after rerun of the events in my mind until I reached a point where I thought I would finally go insane. I could not change events, no matter how hard I tried. My body appeared out of control and I would repeat the same things over and over, witnessing the very same events in a confused psyche and experiencing the same strangely tangled emotions. However, with this constant repetition of events in my mind, perceptions began to shift; the monsters I had battled with appearing somehow different, less monstrous and possibly more human.

In moments of consciousness I could hear Alice's voice, floating in a sea of nothingness. It came to me soft-spoken; a voice filled with sorrow and regret.

"I am so sorry," she said: "I had no choice and I hope that one day you will be freed from this unfortunate fate. I deserve no forgiveness for the pain and suffering you will receive because of me."

The words floated over me, all beyond reach as I kept replaying the events over and over in my mind, losing count of the number of times. More and more my perception of events began to change with almost everyone but Alice and the adventurers looking different, perhaps even distorted, like the very monsters I had killed on my quest. Suddenly I was back in the darkness of the void again and still hearing Alice speaking. This time it was not me she was speaking to. In fact, it sounded like Alaya. I overheard part of what was being said and gradually everything had begun to become much clearer.

I re-lived the events one last time. Darkness swirled around me with the guards appearing completely demonic. The King had suddenly acquired massive horns and glowing red eyes. I made efforts to resist what was happening around me, thinking it must surely be a dark vision consisting of even darker lies, but thoughts even more desperate were telling me that this was probably the truth. Alaya, Axel and Elias had all shifted ever so slightly as we travelled together. So that might have been a sign of sorts. And then, when we fought the minions in the caverns I realised they weren't monsters but men and woman in battered, ineffective armour, all fearful for their lives. In fact, I could now see they were just confused, scared and all fighting in a desperate attempt to survive. When I faced the Demon Lord they had sent me to kill, he looked to me like a knight, wearing a red cloak attached to his worn and rusting plate armour. I could finally understand what he was trying to say.

"Please sir, stop this, think on what you are doing! The demons are tricking you!"

He did his best, but I was too filled with anger to take note of his body language, something that was in reality open, only defensive and perhaps even passive. Such little hints should have made me think twice about what I was doing. Now I finally knew the truth. I couldn't believe it at first, but then I overheard Alice speaking once again.

"The transformation will soon be completed."

It filled me with a mix of anger, fear, pain and sorrow. I fell into a pit of despair.

Then I awoke.

The transformation had been completed successfully, forcing me to experience despair was the last thing needed. That's why they had forced me to re-live my memories. I heard the King call for my execution, but I think that was planned to instil panic and confusion. He had in reality called for my ascension. Everything resembling humanity had been stripped from my physical body. I had transformed into a demonic being, taking on horns and glowing red eyes becoming what they call 'The Fallen Hero'. Alice stayed with me as I tried to wrap my head around what was happening. She explained my mind was still my own but the order of the Demonic King was law. Any order he gives me I must follow. I have no free will of my own any more. I have become a tool, a puppet, a slave and a weapon against the good, mortal kingdoms. Alaya was still alive, and I was shocked to discover she and Elias were one and the same. The strange feeling I got from her, was the effect of her magical ability; a magical body double; a fake person completely. The first time I spoke to the real Alaya had been in my tent on that memorable night.

She avoided me as much as she could, but we had one fateful meeting left before I was forced to leave the castle. It had taken months for my transformation to be completed, seeing her again, meeting her. She was heavily pregnant, at first she didn't realise it was me, but as soon as she did, she left the room in a hurry, appearing visibly upset. A thought crossed my mind, that maybe I was the father, but I couldn't be sure until I remembered what Alice and Alaya spoke about while I was being transformed. Her own words rang heavy on my mind.

"I'm positive it's him, I haven't done it with anyone else in years."

Yet another torturous moment of what would become my new life. Sadly, I doubt I will ever see her again, I will never have the chance to meet my child. This, this hurt more then any torture I had received by far.

My new home was to become 'The Cursed Caverns'; a place I had wished I would never step foot in again. I had no choice. I was forced to wage war and battle armies with my power and with all my might. Alice was assigned to watch over me and she came with me everywhere.

When we were alone, she would apologise profusely, wishing she could disobey the orders of the King. I believed her, despite everything that had happened and despite what she had done. I believed her. She is without doubt a Siren with the magic power of illusion. It was her power that had made me see everyone differently. She didn't look demonic, and to me she was still the most beautiful woman I'd ever seen. She told me she was only half demon, her mother being human, and she was a priestess to the human gods before she was called by the Demon King and enslaved to do his bidding; just like me, I guess! I've killed so many people and with every life taken, I lose myself more and more. The only semblance of peace I have is the time I am alone with Alice. She is in as much pain as me and being just as lonely. If I were still human, we probably would have ended up together. However, we had simply been left to comfort one another and pray all this would end one day.

Soon, I will die having heard rumour of a new Hero being summoned to defeat the demonic armies and push them back. I know the legendary conqueror will arrive here soon, whist on his heroic journey to end the reign of the Demonic King, and to put an end to me, like the sub boss of a video game. I pray he is stronger then the knight I fought in this place, Alice informed me he was another summoned hero from my world.

I welcome the end to come; the end of this living hell.

I have only one hope, that light can be found in the darkest of places. Alice Safare has been my light in this stormy sea of blackness. She isn't evil, nor is she a combatant. She does not deserve to die.

The demonic race is being forced to do the bidding of their King. If someone puts an end to him, she will be freed. She's suffered enough for one lifetime. She blames herself for what happened, I tried to tell her otherwise. I felt the need to give her something, as she wouldn't accept my forgiveness, I asked her, no, told her to survive, to find Alaya and ensure my child's safety. I felt a relief when she accepted.

I hope she will find peace once again; that she will be saved from this nightmare and she can forgive herself for what has happened in the past.

I have decided to document what has happened to me and asked Alice to write a copy in this world's human language too, I have written mine in English for the Hero to read. This is therefore my story and I write it so people will know my suffering and take this as a warning. Maybe, if there are others, by reading this they can be saved.

My name was Zain Fairman, a foolish human who tried to be a hero, only to become a monster known as 'The Fallen Hero'.

PEG POWLER

BY ETHEL STIRMAN

You may be forgiven for missing the cottage altogether. Screened by trees, it remains invisible from the road and only affords the visitor a rare glimpse from the river. Seemingly derelict, its occupant shuns contact with modern society, preferring the safety in isolation.

Once, those living nearby had come to Sarah seeking help: embrocation for an aching back; linctus for a quincied throat; a love charm to ensnare a likely suitor. But times change. Now, brazen in numbers, it is the rough boys who venture forth, seeking her out; throwing sharp stones at her windows; hurling foul-mouthed abuse; torturing her cats. Until, driven by rage, she sallies forth into the lane to heap curses on their heads; promises of retribution.

Sarah and her cottage merge into one: her skin the colour of the ancient stones; her hair matching the straw thatch; her eyes dark as the brooding window panes. No-one can remember a time before Sarah lived at Green Cottage; when she had not been seen gathering sorrel and mushrooms from the hedgerows and woodlands to supplement the herbs growing in her garden.

Now, if their paths chance to cross hers, they draw back. They take care lest her trailing dress of tattered rags should brush against them. They hurry on, not stopping to listen, not trying to make any sense of the incessant mumblings tumbling from her lips.

"Best leave her alone!" mothers instruct their children, but the rough boys do not listen, seeing no danger, only an easy target.

~~~~~~

Early one Spring morning, not long after the sun has risen from its bed, Sarah is in her garden snipping sprigs of lavender, still heavy with dew diamonds, when she feels the earth shudder beneath her bare feet and hears a distant rumble travelling up the river. She raises her head and sniffs the air. Strangers!

All Winter there have been rumours, now, it seems, they have become reality. Men with massive machines will churn up the ground, alter the water course, seek to control the flow of the fastest river in the land. Like Canute, they will endeavour to hold back the tide on its diurnal journey from the North Sea. No good will come of it. Laying her basket of lavender aside, Sarah makes her way to the bottom of the garden to where the river hurries past on its way to the sea. Standing on the bank, she gazes out across the water.

A disturbed moorhen screams in rage as it takes flight from the nearby reeds and a pair of Mallard ducks disdainfully turn their backs and swim further upstream.

Sarah waits while the river settles. A strengthening sun smiles down, warming the land. Cabbage white butterflies dance over the nettle beds and solitary bees buzz around early flowers. Rushing waters speed by, gurgling and splurging through the shallows; silver splinters flashing from ripples. Fish jump in the deep pools. Suddenly, the old woman is alert. There, under the overhanging willow, the first hint of green froth.

Gathering her skirts about her, she hurries back to her cottage. There is much that needs be done and some of the plants she will need grow a long way off.

Way down the Tees, all Summer, the monstrous machines labour, gouging huge channels out of the clay just beyond the river bank. Days turn into weeks; weeks into months; the earth shudders under the effort; the noise deafening, drowning out the wildlife. Men sweat in the heat, suffer in the rain as they grapple with the land, carving an intricate design of channels and basins ready for the damming of the waters.

Only when this great water course is ready will work begin on the great barrage. No trivial dam but a complex system of barrier and flood gates by which the waters can be regulated. Stretching across the river, the concrete base seventy metres wide and thirty-two metres long, supported by five tremendously strong concrete piers. In between these piers, four huge fish belly plates, each measuring eight meters high and weighing fifty tonne, controlling the flow of water, operated by massive hydraulic rams.

The barrage is a magnet for most of the rough boys. As soon as they are freed from school for the weekend, they make their way en masse to the excavations. No signs or wire fences can keep them out; they find ways through the barriers, burrowing or climbing to surmount them like the animals they have become. The site becomes their playground, home to countless adventures, each more dangerous than the last. If they succeed in annoying the workmen enough so that they give chase, so much the better. They are feral and wise in the ways of escaping and quickly re-emerge just out of reach, laughing and gloating.

Sarah welcomes the diversion that keeps them from her door, but she is not plague free. One boy, Jack, somewhat older than the others and therefore a little more dangerous, persists in haunting her. Whenever she ventures into the village, he seems to be waiting, ready to call after her.

'What do you want, old witch? You're not welcome here. Go home to your stinking cottage and look after your mangy cats! Something bad might happen to them.'

The adults turn their heads, ignoring her plight, refusing to acknowledge her shabby treatment at the hands of this young ruffian. Perhaps they welcome any opportunity to deflect Jack's attention away from their door. He follows her home through the lanes, keeping up a stream of verbal abuse and often lifting great clods of weeds and soil from the ditches to hurl at her back. She flinches each time one hits its mark, but never turns to face him, intent on chanting under her breath.

Usually, he gives up before they arrive at her gate but once or twice he has lingered by the garden's boundary fence, throwing stones at her windows, catching a cat if he gets the chance, making it scream like some unearthly demon before releasing it, spitting and scratching, claws extended.

Sarah watches him, muttering incoherently, only a single word decipherable: Jack.

When she is certain he has gone, she picks up her basket and makes her way down to the water's edge. An ancient wooden jetty allows her access to the river's surface. She stares deep into the water, beyond the glinting ripples, to where the fishes glide majestically amongst the reeds, their sinuous bodies never at rest in the fast-flowing stream.

Chanting, she carefully selects from her basket, strewing leaves and flowers over the surface: comfrey, sage and garlic for protection; fennel to ward off curses. After each herb she says, 'Protect my home and all within. Protect all those free from sin.'

After the offering has disappeared out of sight, Sarah again stares deep into the water. Down, down, down, the weeds swirl like green tresses in the current. She cannot be certain but for a moment a face appears, its eyes staring back, full of hate and despair. Sarah shivers and it is gone but she is not fooled. Men are playing at gods, altering the nature of the river. There will be a price to pay.

~~~~~~

Late in the Summer, as the great works are nearing completion, there is a noticeable change in the river. Across the water's surface huge swathes of thick green frothy scum appear, whirling and churning, caught in the eddies under the banksides. Mothers keep their children close; rumours abound about Peg Powler's Suds and the High Green Ghost famed for dragging children into the river to drown. One or two even consider a trip to Sarah's cottage but their shame keeps them away.

One dark moonless night, Sarah mixes mugwort in her pestle, sets it alight and breathes deeply of the vapours as they rise. In a trance-like state, she journeys once more down to the river and gazes deep into the dark waters. She stares beyond the here and now, seeking to discover what will be. Her face reflects the visions she sees: sometimes in pain, sometimes in pleasure. At last she is certain what her course must be. Waking, a smile upon her lips, she sets off swiftly towards the village.

Jack is occupied trying to break into the back of the General Dealers on the High Street. He is alone, has no intention of sharing his spoils with the younger boys. Pride swells his chest; there have been several break-ins lately but the local bobby has failed to even come close to apprehending the thief. Having honed his skills, this should be the most lucrative job to date.

He has almost managed to prise away the lock, when the hairs on the back of his neck stand up as he becomes aware of someone approaching the end of the back lane. He sinks back into the shadows, his hoodie hiding his fair hair, waiting for the uninvited guest to pass. His eyes light up as the stranger is illuminated by the street light on the corner. 'It is that old witch, Sarah Green,' he thinks. 'Now what is she up to?' He sets off to follow her; the shop can wait: there's always another night.

It takes all her strength of purpose to stop Sarah from turning round to check the boy is following her. The soft-soled sneakers he wears stifle his footsteps and for once he does not call after her. But she is confident that he will not be able to pass up his chance to bait her. She continues down the street.

Good, Jack smiles, they are heading for the bridge. Soon they will leave most of the houses behind; there will be fewer adults about to spoil his fun. His grin broadens as he imagines the ways he will torment the old lady; pity she has none of her cats with her; he'd like to see them drown.

They are close now to her destination but instead of carrying on over the bridge, Sarah turns aside and makes for the tow path below it, which pleases Jack even more. In the darkest shadows she halts and stretching her hands out over the rushing waters, she begins to chant. Under the bridge, there is an eerie green light emanating from the mass of green foam gathering by side of the river.

For the first time, Jack begins to feel uneasy as Sarah turns to face him, her face showing no fear; her eyes boring deep into him, to his very soul.

'Here we are then, Jack. What happens now is up to you. Leave at once or stay and face the consequences of your actions.'

He hesitates momentarily, shakes his head in disbelief at his own timidity, then begins to walk towards her determinedly. Too late he hears the boiling of the waters; too late he sees the figure rise from amongst the green foam, verdant tresses flying about grotesque features in an ancient face; too late to escape the skeletal claw as it wraps around his ankle and pulls him into the water. His final terrifying memory, the sharpened teeth glinting in her silent triumphant screams she drags him down screaming into the maelstrom of weeds below, wrapped in the arms of Peg Powler, High Green Ghost of the Tees.

Sarah makes her way slowly home. Two birds with one stone, she thinks. Jack's reign of terror is ended, and the river deity has her sacrifice. Peace will be restored but only so long as the river lies undisturbed.

ALTERNATIVE MEDICINE

BY
KEVIN HORSLEY

It was late October in 1870 when we heard from a reliable friend of newly discovered gold at a wild and savage frontier called Botswana in Southern Africa. My husband Henry wasted no time and arranged an expedition.

By January all was in order and we set sail from Plymouth. We arrived some weeks later at Cape Town, having briefly stopped off at Verde Islands to re-provision and carry out some small repairs to our vessel.

Upon arrival we spent a few days in preparation for the land journey across the lush natural landscape of the region. I recall that the expedition to Botswana was not without its perils. At times it seemed the landscape and indigenous species were working in tandem against us, slowing our progress. We had to take a detour around a herd of elephants and the insects lazed around in swarms, like heavy rain-filled clouds, buzzing menacingly and attacking us if they were disturbed.

Eventually we arrived at our destination where Henry and his team erected some simple fortifications around our encampment and the prospectors went about their business of determining the best place to mine for the precious gold.

The whole thing was a bit of a disaster and, through providence, we were lucky to break even on the entire affair upon our return home some four months later.

~~~~~~

We had been back at home in England for no more than a week when it began; a throbbing in my temples and stabbing pains in my abdomen. I thought nothing of it for a day or two. It was perhaps a little more severe than usual, but then the fever came. My body felt as though it were on fire and no matter how little clothing I wore, for I had to protect my modesty, the heat did not abate.

I do not know for how long the fever had raged through my body, all I know is that it must have been for quite an alarming amount of time. Henry had spent a good deal of time and money on doctors in an attempt to find a cure for my malady. A curious blight most probably of African origin, passed on from those swarms of biting insects.

In any event, my fever became so bad that I was taken to incoherent ranting before becoming placid and returning to a state of unconsciousness.

Henry loved me dearly and I suspect that he would have sacrificed almost anything for me to return to an improved state of health, which is why he did what he did, for better or for worse.

In his desperation to find a cure he was made aware of a professor who had made claims he could cure any disease, albeit by unorthodox means. It was spoken of in whispers and was said to be so expensive that only the crème de la crème could afford such a treatment, the nature of which was not revealed.

Well, this smattering of hope was all that Henry needed. He swiftly made the arrangements and we travelled during the night to a remote country home by carriage; the horses directed by Henry and not our usual driver being part of the agreement required by the mysterious professor. I slipped into the comfort of dreamless sleep for the journey.

Upon arrival, Henry helped me out of the carriage and mostly carried me in my weakened state. We could see that the residence was a tall modern structure set within ample grounds. It appeared tranquil and peaceful in the twilight. There was a stable, but no stable boy which was surprising but understandable, in keeping with the conditions surrounding this particular endeavour.

Henry raised the large iron knocker, fashioned into the shape of a lion's head, and banged three times onto the solid mahogany door; the sound echoing within the confines of the house. Henry, in his impatience and worry, was about to knock again but a shuffling sound saw him relax and place the knocker gently down.

A moment later the sturdy door opened silently revealing a tall man in a tweed jacket holding a gas lit lamp in his right hand.

The light made him appear other-worldly, his face reflected the light which obscured most of his features making his eyes appear to be pits of darkness.

'You must be Henry' he said in a serious and gravelly voice.

'And you must be the professor' Henry replied hurriedly 'Quickly man, help me get her inside'.

The professor stooped down and lifted me easily. He had a faint unpleasant smell about him but I put this down to the tweed jacket.

There was an underlying musky odour and some other unidentifiable scents, vaguely unpleasant, which must have been related to his work.

'Henry, my good man, do not be worried. Your lovely wife is in good hands and I will see that she is lain in comfort and attended to. You will need to take care of the horses as I have no man-servants on duty to help'.

'Horses be damned, I'm not leaving her side.'

'As you would have it but be aware that you cannot be present for the treatment, I cannot allow it. Your health would be at risk, but ask me to reveal nothing more just yet. Come let us not tarry here any longer.'

With those words spoken we entered into the large reception hall which was dimly lit by gas lamps, one at either side of the room.

My beloved Henry closed the door quietly and hurried to keep pace with the long strides of the strange professor. We entered into the guest lounge which was better lit by a crystal chandelier raised four yards up and attached to the ceiling by slim metallic chains.

There was a mahogany bookshelf with numerous leather bound titles on the far wall and a coffee table in the centre of the room with four solid, high backed armchairs all fashioned from the same dark wood, the chairs cushioned and embroidered in the oriental designs of flying dragons.

A coal fireplace was located in the centre of the right hand wall, the iron grill charred black, behind the fire and beneath the mahogany mantle piece was a slab of black marble. The hearth was of the same material and on the mantle-piece were rosewood carvings of large faced imps wearing snarls and sneers which seemed particularly sinister in the flickering firelight.

Placed on the hearth was an iron container of intricate spirals for the tongs and poker. Next to the fire, immediately to the right of the entrance into this room, was a drinks cabinet which matched the rest of the décor. Oddly there were no ornaments or portraits or other works of art within the room. It seemed to lack something, in spite of the elegant furnishings.

'Please be seated here good sir, I will take your wife to her room and return here shortly so we can discuss the matter of payment. For now feel free to help yourself to a snifter of brandy from the decanter on the cabinet over there by the fireplace'.

With that I heard my darling Henry shuffle across to the drinks cabinet, the clack of a door closing and then the clink of crystal on crystal.

I heard the door close behind me and strained to see in the poor illumination afforded only by candlelit lamps. I thought that the air seemed colder the further we travelled down the corridor but that could be my sickness, I felt alone without Henry and oh so vulnerable.

'Professor' I said weakly

He replied softly, yet sternly.

'Hush now my dear, save your strength. There will be time for discussion and introductions later'.

Truth be told, I did not have the strength to argue and so took this small advice. We stopped as he opened another door, then guided me into a darker room and I was even more reliant on the lamplight.

This new room felt dreadfully cold and had a musty scent to it that reminded me of an earthy enclosure. I also heard the rattling scrape of something metal in one of the far corners of the room and something that hissed inwardly like a sharp inhalation of air. I began to feel nauseous with fear but considered that I was having another episode due to this awful illness.

As the professor neared me I let out a whimper to which he soothed.

'There, there my lady. I need to move you onto the bed for comfort before I can begin'.

I nodded, my eyes stinging feverishly. He bent over and placed one warm hand beneath my knees, the other behind my head and lifted me with relative ease. I noticed that pungent smell again with the lesser odours attempting to fight their way out as he gently swayed me across to the bed and placed me delicately onto the soft mattress. His final action was the careful removal of my silver cross necklace which he placed with a jangle onto a metal tray atop the bedside table, no doubt also mahogany I mused.

The scraping sound seemed closer and more erratic, and the professor moved out of the lamplight to somewhere else in the room. There was then a shuffling motion as though something laboured toward me. I struggled to turn my head as I felt a presence next to me and the air had reached the frigid proportions of a bitter winter morning.

In the dim light was a pallid face hovering near to me. It looked at me with watered blue eyes which bore into me and I felt my will weaken further, the lips were thin and bloodless and I was unable to determine the gender of the creature that was a mockery of humanity. Around the neck of the abomination was a collar that shone faintly in the light, though I was unsure of the metal. It lifted a pale talon-like hand up which also had a chain of the same metal around the wrist. Raising a slender finger to its lips it motioned for me to shush. I don't know what power came over me but I felt calm, relaxed even and sighed as I looked away.

Its hand was placed on my throat and I did not flinch, not even in reflex, at how frigid it was. Even as it brushed my long curled blond hair aside, expelling the warmth that my lustrous locks afforded me. Then I felt an even deeper frigidity on my neck and heard a slight gurgle escape from its mouth. Time stood still for what seemed like an eternity until I felt the press of its frozen lips against my exposed skin before an ecstatic fire coursed through my being up to the pinnacle of the now penetrated flesh. Like a volcano, the heat gushed and flowed and was all that existed in the world.

I groaned like I was experiencing ecstasy for the first time, but intensified ten-fold. My back arched as the feeling reached its peak and then I slowly lay myself back down into the enveloping softness of the bed, feeling absolutely spent. I slept with a contented smile for the first time since the sickness began.

I cannot begin to tell you how brazen I felt later once the realisation of what had happened occurred to me, I decided there and then that my beloved Henry could never learn of this.

The professor brusquely woke me and I felt that I had barely rested at all, but he impressed upon me with urgency that I drink down the draught of medicine he had prepared.

Handing me the carved crystal goblet, I noticed its warmth through the engravings and a slight spicy aroma. Drinking it down was difficult at first, for it was a thick viscous liquid that left a faint metallic after taste, but I persisted and gagged it down.

I lay back down and passed back into the dark comfort of unconsciousness.

When I next awoke, this time at no one's insistence but my own need to awaken, I felt rejuvenated and more alive than I had felt in months.

Immediately I noticed the soothing scent of lavender in the air, it was a welcome comfort that offered the familiarity of home. It was only when I opened my eyes that I realised the truth of it, I was home and safely tucked up in my own bed.

Forgetting myself, I quickly arose and went straight over to the oval mirror on my dresser. I was concerned that the illness had ravaged my natural beauty, but was pleasantly surprised to see that I looked better than I had in a long time.

The tanned skin from the excursion to Africa had gone and my complexion was paler than ever, the dark shadows beneath my eyes had disappeared as had the wrinkles brought on by the exhaustion.

I was almost porcelain made flesh. The relief that my vanity was satisfied was overwhelming and I began to laugh. The sound was like the sweetest music in the world.

My laughter was interrupted by a knock on the door, I recovered myself and asked loudly:

'Who is it?'.

'Tis Ella milady, is everything alright?'

Ella was our most trusted housekeeper, both motherly yet diligent in her undertakings, and I had no doubt that she would also have been worried for me.

'Oh Ella, yes, yes it is. Please fetch Henry. I really need to see him' I said smiling broadly.

She replied excitedly:

'Of course milady' and hurried away. I imagined that she curtsied outside of the door prior to her departure; her loyalty to us knew no bounds.

Climbing back into bed I propped my pillows up and sat waiting for my wonderful husband to arrive, I did not have long to wait as he practically barged into my room.

He stood there looking at me a little out of breath, his mouth hanging agape.

I needed to hold him, to kiss him, to tell him I loved him. The concern in his eyes melted as I wrapped my arms around him and placed my lips upon his, hungering for him and the physical confirmation that I was alive and all was going to be well.

It was only after a few moments that we realised Ella was stood there in the doorway, tears of relief streaming down her aged face to the edges of her smiling mouth.

Looking into Henry's eyes I could see the desire burning away, I regained my composure a little and turned to Ella.

'Ella my dear, would you be so good as to prepare us some breakfast.'

Both Henry and Ella looked at me a little strangely.

'What, what is it?' I questioned a little embarrassed.

Henry smirked: 'But darling, it's nearly four in the afternoon'.

'Oh' I exclaimed: 'is it really, oh my. Well, that will do me fine then, please leave me to dress and I will join you promptly for dinner'.

With that, Ella left us and I had another passionate clinch with Henry. As he was leaving he turned to me, puppy dog eyes pleading for more. With a smile I dismissed him and turned to ready myself.

I half walked, half danced to the window and drew back the black velvet curtains to bask in whatever light remained, it felt glorious to be alive.

The light hurt my eyes and made my head thrum. I quickly stepped back and closed the curtains while shielding my face with an upraised arm.

My skin tingled where the blazing light had touched and my eyes continued to burn, tears flowed but did nothing to stop the irritation.

I lay upon the bed and buried my face into the duvet, trying not to weep with the shock.

How silly of me, I thought, to look out into daylight when I had not been exposed to it for such a long time, I mean, I did not even know the date so did not know how much time had elapsed. Such little impracticalities that I must learn to overcome on the road to recovery.

Henry found me like this and coaxed me up gently, I asked him simply to ensure all the rooms leading to the dining room were candlelit.

He looked worried when he saw my bloodshot eyes and kissed the tears from my cheeks, but agreed to do as I had asked.

Unperturbed, I got out of bed and lit the gas lamp on my dresser, put on my luxurious tea-dress and brushed my silken locks up into a bun. I then used some of the scent Henry had brought back from one of his many business trips. As I gracefully descended the stairs to the dining area, the flames of the candles flickered casting erratic shadows onto the walls making it appear that the silhouettes were chasing one another in a perpetual game of cat and mouse.

Henry ensured I was seated before taking his place at the head of the table, he rang the servants bell for attendance.

The first course was celery soup. I found it a little rich but managed most of it and the heat of it filled my stomach initially satisfying me, but knew I would need something more .

Fish in white sauce with a side of boiled vegetables followed and I managed a few mouthfuls before I could consume no more. I was beginning to feel sickly and clamminess coated my skin.

I made my apologies and left Henry insisting I would be fine, I had just had too much too soon.

Almost stumbling up the stairs to the bathroom, I vomited all that I had eaten into the water closet and flushed it all away. I dazedly made my way to the bedroom, my stomach cramping in agony and I did not know why.

I could hear Henry speaking to Ella but not what was said, their garbled speech formed a soothing rhythm that sent me to sleep. I awoke to Henry stroking my forehead and hair. His hands felt rough and his face looked troubled.

'Oh Henry, What is wrong with me?'

'I am afraid, my dear, that you are weaker than we had thought. Maybe you need a little more time to recover your strength properly. Would you like me to fetch a little broth to help soothe your hunger?'

'No my darling, could you stay here with me while I rest and watch over me?'

'Of course I can, but I just need to relieve Ella for the evening. There's nothing more she can do tonight.'

'Please be quick Henry dear, I have missed you so much and need you here with me.'

Slowly he got up from the bed, gently laying me down and covering me. He seemed to hesitate as he looked at me, then smiled weakly and left.

His footsteps caused a staccato on the stairs, a swift rhythm echoing in the darkness.

I was not alone for long, Henry returned and lay with me my back to him, I could feel his breath against my neck cooling and soothing as I fell asleep.

The pain returned to my stomach, it felt like a tightly clenched hand squeezing my insides into a ball and I cried out into the darkened room sitting upright, awake and despairing.

Henry was immediately beside me, holding me and whispering that everything was going to be fine.

I turned to him, seeking the protection of his body and looked into his eyes the worry etched into his eyes which squinted in the darkness. I traced my finger around his cupids bow and kissed him, his eyes lit up with pleasant surprise and he reciprocated, holding me close, kissing me back. I yielded to him needing the closeness of the flesh. I was lost in that moment, and it is only now I bitterly regret losing myself so entirely for maybe I could have avoided what happened next. Maybe ...

Time stopped in that moment, it ceased to exist in the throes of passion and what I felt was all consuming. I was aware of nothing but the need. I was being driven to the inevitable that I could not possibly foresee.

My heart thundered less rapidly, my pulse began to slow and my mind was clearing. The agony that had gripped my stomach was gone, a distant memory of an era nearly forgotten. Opening my eyes, I could see Henry laying there spent from our exertions, I wondered just how long our lost moment had lasted.

It occurred to me that he was laying in what must have been an uncomfortable position so I attempted to move him, finding this to be much easier than I could have ever thought in my weakened state, his skin felt cool to the touch and his breath rattled in his chest like that of a diseased or aged man.

Worriedly I nudged him. 'Henry, wake up. Please Henry, you are scaring me.'

His breath hung for a moment before the lengthy exhalation I now know was his last. 'Henry, Henry, what is wrong?' I was hysterical and could not think straight. 'Henry.' I screamed over and over and over.

'Wake up.'

While sobbing I glanced over to the mirror on my dresser and saw my darkened eyes, with deep red streaks running down my cheeks, my lips a deep scarlet colour smudged around the edges and a pink mark on my chin. I looked more intensely at my reflection and moved closer, horrified by what I could see, it was blood. I was crying blood.

I went back to Henry and examined my beautiful husband. He was entirely limp, his skin pale and statuesque, his hair tousled around a face fixed in contentment. There was a small red stain on the pillow under his head. I moved this gently to one side and gasped when I saw the damson mark on his neck, much like when sucking at your wrist to leave a welt only with two deep puncture marks evenly spaced in parallel.

It made me feel sick and I wretched, a gout of viscous metallic fluid entered my mouth and into my nasal cavity causing me to gag.

But the metallic taste caused my stomach to stir again, caused my limbs to ache with need and I swallowed instinctively which sickened me further.

What was happening to me and how could I go on without my loving and caring Henry.

I sat. Time passed. Seconds became minutes and minutes became an hour; the world continued to turn. The ticking of the grandfather clock in the hall matched the cruel beating of my heart and slowly my mind began to work.

Henry was dead. I was responsible for his death. I had murdered him and I was condemned to die for what I had done.

Unless ... Unless, I could bring him back!

Maybe there was a chance. I had been weak, to the point of death. Everyone had given up on me except my sweet heart.

I vaguely remembered the coach journey, a strange house an even stranger host and something else, something that my mind didn't want me to know. I could feel it scratching at the surface of my consciousness like a distant nightmare that has fled with the daylight.

Resorting to finding my beloveds diary, I ran to his room and searched his desk where one of the drawers was locked. The deep mahogany with brass fittings remained unyielding to my efforts to open it. The key must be with Henry! I ran back and checked his pockets. I felt ashamed but this was a necessity. I found the keys for our home as well as some smaller ones for the gun cabinet and his desk.

The drawer opened; his diary was within and I read through the events of the past months realising that we were now in July. It was summertime, meaning it would be daylight in a matter of hours. I could not afford another attack like the one that had happened earlier that evening when the once blessed warmth of the sun on my skin caused such a bad reaction.

Finally I found a small entry of his first visit to the mysterious Professor including the address and what had transpired at that meeting.

He had left me totally in the care of this man and waited for a day and a half for me to show some signs of recovery. It mentioned his concerns for me and the worry he felt. My heart was beating more rapidly and I could feel my eyes welling up again for my beloved.

I did not have time for this sentimentality and quickly dressed in some of the hard wearing garments I had worn all those months ago when we went to South Africa. They would help to mask my femininity.

All of the serving staff were away which was fortunate. I swiftly wrote a letter for Ella describing how we were going away for a couple of days. It would be a holiday away from all the recent concerns and we would be back soon. I grabbed some clothes of his and mine; some other necessities, some money, a brace of pistols from the cabinet and the pillow with the stains on it.

In less than an hour we were on our way to see the Professor which was something of a surprise for me as I usually spent hours pampering myself for readiness.

I was unexpected and uninvited but I had purpose and my demeanour was set.

~~~~~~

The journey was thankfully without incident and the horses slowed as we arrived at the manor house. I must say I was impressed by the immensity of the grounds.

Tethering the horses to a nearby post I ran to the door and banged upon it with my fists. I listened intently for a few seconds and then hammered on the door again.

Finally I could discern slow, steady footsteps walking across a wooden floor and the door rattled and opened silently.

A familiar looking man was stood there holding a gas lit lamp. He was tall and gaunt and clearly the same man who had nursed me back to health.

'Good evening Professor, I need your help.' I gasped breathily.

Looking me up and down he sighed as he said with irritation 'How did you find me?'

'Does that really matter? My husband is gravely ill with something, maybe the same thing that made me sick and I need your help. Will you at least look at him?'

'Madam, I sincerely doubt he has what afflicted you because he would have displayed symptoms of it far earlier than now. However, I will do as you bid and have a look. If I can help I will, for a fee of course.'

He smiled as he said this, his teeth like yellow slabs in the dark cavern of his mouth.

We both went to the carriage and retrieved Henry, slowly carrying him into the house so as not to make him suffer any further discomfort. He felt cold and inflexible as we lay him down onto one of the couches in the lounge area which seconded as a waiting area.

The Professor got a medical kit out and used a stethoscope first.

'Hmm'

He then opened an eyelid and looked into the eye.

'Yes, it is just as I had thought.'

'What is it, can you help?'

The Professor stepped back and looked at me gravely.

'I am afraid there is nothing I can do for your husband. He is no longer with us. I would estimate he passed a few hours ago.'

'No, you must help him, he did everything he could to help me. I cannot live without him.'

I could feel the hysteria climbing up my spine like a slowly ascending wave of cold fear threatening to overwhelm me. I fought it down and looked at the Professor with steel in my eyes.

'Can you not give him the elixir you gave me to help me get back to health?'

'My dear lady, there is nothing I can do for him it is too late even for the elixir. I cannot bring back the dead. My miracle cure only works on the living. Once the spark has gone, it cannot be re-ignited.'

The despair had its claws out again and they were tearing into me. I clenched my teeth.

'Please can you try it anyway? I will pay you handsomely for it.'

'I am sorry but I must refuse. It is precious and cannot be wasted. Not for any price.'

I could see that I was getting nowhere with this stubborn man, so I did the only thing I could. I pulled one of the pistols out and pointed it at him.

He gasped when he saw what I was wielding and moved away from me slowly, but there was nowhere for him to hide.

'I did not want this to happen, I was hoping you would be more helpful but the life of my husband is more important to me than all the wealth we have, do you think that your life means anything to me when compared to that?'

'There really is no need to pull a gun out on me; I mean you might hurt yourself.'

BOOM!

I fired a warning shot into the drinks cabinet to his right, ruining a perfectly good decanter of Brandy. I smiled without humour

'Do not make me use this on you, I would not want to miss my target and hit something you really need.' I motioned towards his face. He held his hands up in defeat.

'Alright, alright you win, I concede. Just wait here while I go and retrieve some of the elixir for you.'

'Do you take me for a simpleton Professor? I may not be as learned as you but I am no fool either. No, you will take me with you.'

'So be it.'

With that he opened the door at the other end of the room and I quickly followed, keeping the muzzle pointed directly at him.

The solid mahogany door clicked shut behind me and the Professor made his way down the corridor. It must have been cold down there because I could see his breath misting in the air ahead of him. Even though there was very little light I could see perfectly clearly and we passed a closed door on the left; another solid dark wood door with a mortise lock.

We got to the end of the corridor. The Professor hesitated and glanced around.

I motioned to the door with the gun.

'Open it.'

He pulled out a key. It scraped inside the lock and the door creaked open. He slowly stepped inside the room and I followed, ensuring a healthy distance between us.

Upon entering the room I could see an old hospital bed with chains and padlocks attached to it. I knew that this was the bed I was placed into when I had first been brought here those few nights ago.

There was a scraping noise coming from the distance in the room just like last time and my attention diverted to it before I could stop myself. In that moment the Professor acted. While distracted my right arm was struck and was jolted.

BOOM!

The gun fired and I saw sparks in the distance followed by a fearful yelp. Numbness coursed down to my hand and the gun dropped from lifeless fingers. The sound of the gunfire echoed around the room and the acrid gun-smoke filled the air, burning my eyes. The yelp became a whimpering sound and I could see a greyish shape shambling slowly towards us.

I looked at the Professor who was holding a wooden cane with a skull hand grip. This was some kind of metal, silver maybe. He was holding the silver coloured tip of the opposite end and wielding it like a club, he looked at me warily and I smiled before I lunged for the pistol. My eyes had betrayed me and looked at the gun just moments before I made a move for it. He had anticipated this and swung his weapon with unerring accuracy, hitting me across the jaw-line. I felt bones break and dislocate. The pain was excruciating. It felt like an explosion had gone off inside my head. I was left shocked and unable to react. I was falling as another attack thudded dully into my left shoulder and I collapsed to the floor.

Out of the corner of my eye I saw the greyish humanoid form leap at the professor. There was a collar around its neck and a piece of broken chain waved in the air as it descended.

The Professor was taken by surprise and stumbled over, I grabbed an arm without thinking and could feel the precious blood pumping through his veins; the sound of it bringing me back to my surroundings.

I could feel the bones in my face knitting back together. It was not painful but more of a discomfort.

My teeth grew out slowly and the hunger was upon me once more. I savagely bit into his wrist sparing no mercy and stared into his eyes as I drank.

His blood did not taste like Henry's had, it was thicker and more delicious, it was better than the finest wine I had ever drank and I was delirious with intoxication.

My gaze never lost contact with his eyes the whole time. It stopped me from losing myself again. I wanted him to know that I knew what I was doing.

I did not enjoy watching the light fade from his eyes, nor did I feel remorse either, for what was this death after the loss of my beloved.

I realised I had to accept that Henry was truly gone from me. This realisation caused pain; it caused anguish and I felt as though my heart would rupture and burst from my chest.

Blood tears flowed once more with the agony of it, the grief I felt for my darling who would never be by my side again.

Movement near the prostrate form of the Professor brought me back to the real situation and my grieving would be forced to wait for later.

The greyish form was almost corpse-like and emaciated beyond belief. It took me a moment of deduction to realise that this was once a man. However, his skin colour of a light mottled brown betrayed the fact that he was no native to English soil.

'Who, who are you?' I managed to croak out.

He opened his mouth, stained with the same blood that I had drank, to reveal he had no tongue, he motioned for me to come closer and although he was monstrous to me he had saved me from certain death.

Reluctantly I moved forward, he held both hands up in a gesture which implied he was not threatening me and slowly moved his right hand towards my face and placed a palm against my temple.

I received a flash of images, too quick for me to make sense of, and he looked at me eagerly.

He could see the puzzled expression on my face so tried again, this time the imagery was much slower.

It showed him, back when he was human and of Asian stock. He had left his family to go hunting and become lost in the wilderness.

In the dark of the night with only the moon for illumination he had become the hunted. A terrifying figure had descended from the trees and knocked him to the floor. The figure revealed a set of razor sharp teeth glinting menacingly in the filtered moonlight and sank them into the throat of the frightened man.

The fear I could feel from these memories made me feel claustrophobic. My throat constricted involuntarily and I gagged.

The next image showed the figure drawing a knife across his wrist, the blood was a black colour and flowed into the open mouth of the man who had been attacked; the man showing me these images.

I understood that this was the creation of what he now was, of what I now am; that the elixir was actually blood, a special kind of blood.

The rest of the images showed his own discovery that daylight was harmful. His arm remained blackened and limp for months and his face scarred for a longer period of time, though this had healed eventually.

I learned that he had been captured by the Professor and subjected to many experiments. The Professor had regularly drank of this creature but had never become like him.

This made me realise that maybe a human in perfect health could drink this blood, my blood, and become stronger and fitter and more alive; the perfect elixir of health. So how had I become what I now was, had I truly been that close to death?

Lastly I gleaned from the images that this pitiful creature no longer wanted to go on. He wanted to be released so that he may finally rest.

In the image he showed me baring my fangs and sinking them into him, it showed the expression on his face to be one in utter bliss as he finally slumped against me.

I looked at him in some measure of understanding. He had suffered enough and it was either me benefitting by drinking from him, or him waiting for the sun to rise and venture out to embrace it once final time.

He got his final wish. I was gentle. I treated him like a lover and I was grateful for both occasions when he had saved my life. His blood was like nothing I had ever tasted, even more potent than that of the Professor and I got a flood of memories and emotions that I otherwise would never have known. He gave all he could freely before slowly disintegrating into the cold stone floor.

I felt the sympathy hit me when I saw the ash and dust of all that remained of him. How much he must have despised this state of being to want to leave it so desperately.

The Professor's body seemed to have aged many years since his demise. He had originally appeared to be a man in his late forties but now he was a haggard and twisted form and appeared to be in his late nineties.

'So the blood also helps to preserve youth' I found myself wondering. The dawn swiftly approached but I had one last thing to do before it arrived and forced me to hide.

I went to Henry. I kissed him tenderly on the lips, the nose, the forehead and then bit my wrist to release the life giving elixir. It dripped slowly into his open mouth and proceeded to accumulate in the cavity until it flowed out and down his chin.

That was the instant my heart truly broke; the instant I knew I could never have him again, smell him, touch him, feel him or see him smile.

I did not lose it like I thought I might, I cleaned up the mess I (he) had made and left for the darkened room.

It was unsettling to remain in there but for now it would have to do. I would find something better tomorrow. Right now I needed to rest and recuperate.

The following night, I transferred Henry's body to an area of the town which was disreputable. I had to stab a knife into him and spill some more blood, to make it appear to be a fresh kill and left him there to be discovered in a darkened alley.

I myself returned home. I deliberately made myself dishevelled and sought out Ella.

Describing to her how we had been attacked and how Henry had been so brave to stop them from stealing my jewels and told me to run. How I had seen him beat one of them down and the others run away. He had given chase, I begged him to stop but he would not listen, could not hear me above the need for retribution.

How I had fled and returned here to the house only to find Ella here. I was hysterical.

Ella did her best to comfort me and I made my excuses to retire once daylight approached. The following evening saw the police arrive. I gave descriptions of the three vagabonds (two of which matched the Asian and the Professor albeit in ragged clothing) who were clearly desperate to accost Henry and I on our way home.

I gave them details of the locale. It was the outskirts of a well known bad place but still we should have been safe.

They thanked me for my time. I knew their investigations would reveal nothing more and it would be written off in a week or so if I did not pursue them

Poor Henry! His body was discovered two days later by the police. It had been reported that day by some unfortunate old dear on her way back from the local bakery. She was still in shock the police informed me. I thanked them for the information and looked away, pretending to be aloof and numb with grief.

They left with promises of how they would catch the bastard who did this. I nodded my encouragement and left Ella to attend to the funeral arrangements. I could not attend the funeral, so pretended to get very drunk, keeping Ella up until the very early hours and ensuring she too was inebriated.

When she came to rouse me from my slumber, she could not; not even by candle or lamplight.

And so hidden behind the façade of drunken grief I escaped the funeral and all the family members who would be there to offer condolences, people who had never visited us once in the five years we had lived together in matrimonial bliss.

Henry had left me everything in the will, which I promptly sold with the excuse of too many memories. Some of Henry's male relations had suddenly become much friendlier. It was disgusting, but I kept a note of those who felt the need to sully the memory of my good husband.

Ella was given a handsome amount of money for her dedication and services. I do not know what became of her once she moved away. I left her with the best of wishes as she cried her thanks and appreciation.

I returned to the Professor's secluded house. If anything was amiss it would have been discovered and reported by now. Everything was as I had left it.

The Professor had earned a shallow grave on his land. It was left unmarked. The house I had decorated, according to my tastes, and I spared no expense.

My plans were to continue the work of the Professor. I would provide the elixir of life to those who could afford it. I knew that what I offered was pure, was controlled and was safe.

I would be offering an alternative medicine.

FISHING TRIP

BY
KEVIN HORSLEY

Machk stands within the stillness of the lake, the water to his knees. The glaring Sun beats down upon his tanned body, poised with his spear held in the air, the obsidian tip angled towards the surface of the lake.

A bead of sweat forms on his forehead and makes the slow journey to the crest of his right eyebrow and gathers. As the bead fattens and grows heavy Machk remains perfectly still until the spear moves in one fluid motion, splashing into the water and out again. A salmon flaps in its death throes on the end of the weapon and sunlight shimmers across its silver armour.

'Achak my son, catch!'

Machk deftly removes the fish and tosses it over to Achak who waits at the edge of the gently lapping water. He catches it and places it into a woven basket with some other fish.

'One more son and we can begin; start on the fire.'

Machk resumes his position while Achak moves away to gather wood for the fire.

In the distance a coyote howls, the call makes the ears of Machk prick up; the coyote knows what is coming he thinks.

Achak gets the fire started and hears a series of splashes, then sees his father striding out of the water towards him.

'Won't be long now son.' he says calmly as he starts to roast one of the fish on the fire.

They each eat to their hearts content and smoke the others for their return to the tribe.

'Why are we here father?'

'Now is the time of your coming of age. You will soon be a man. I have a story to tell, the same story that my father told me and his father told him and so on back to the beginnings of our people.'

Sitting onto the rough, shale like ground he begins to tell his tale.

'Back when the world was young and newly made, Man and Beast ran as equals across the vast plains and the high mountains. Bird held his domain in the open sky and Fish held his place in the watery depths.

The valley you see before you was a verdant paradise where Man did not have to hunt to survive for the trees and bushes bore many fruits, nuts and berries all year round.

Sun and Moon worked in harmony and our lives were simpler than they are now, we worked together with the land, Bird, Beast and Fish, and all were content.

We paid Sun and Moon homage for their provisions and on occasions when the two would meet in the sky, turning day into night, we would all get together and celebrate their union with feasting, and it was a deemed to be a fertile time, so many couplings took place. We all lived in harmony; Bird flew, Fish swam, Beast hunted. Man learned and developed, but we all assisted each other.

It was approaching the time when Sun and Moon would once again meet after a very long time and Man had found new ways to honour them. We had learned to dance and taught these dances to all. We had learned to use different berries and leaves for paints and drew on the mountain images of all their creations living in blessed union.

All was well until Coyote became jealous of Man and knew that Sun and Moon would be awestruck by the artwork Man had created to venerate them. So he hatched a plan to stop Man from becoming favourite.

He turned his back on Sun and hid in the shade of the mountain caves during the daytime. Then, when the world slept, he would slink from shadow to shadow until he reached the mountainous peaks and would pay homage to Moon only.

At first Sun did not notice that Coyote was missing, busy as he was ensuring that the world was nourished. Coyote had grown lazy and accustomed to sleeping until the twilit hours and did not realise that the time where day became as dark as night was upon him.

When Sun met with Moon they looked out upon the host before them and immediately saw that Coyote was missing, Sun was furious that Coyote was not there to offer thanks and questioned the other creatures but no one, other than Vulture, knew of Coyote's whereabouts.

Cruel old Vulture flew higher and higher to sow the seeds of chaos and spoke with Sun of all he had seen, of how many moons had passed since Coyote had last let sunlight warm his body. He hoped to benefit from Coyotes downfall.

This only infuriated Sun further and his anger grew, he demanded of Moon why she did not tell him and would not listen to her when she said that she did not know, for the daytime was not her domain.

The two of them argued for much longer than their normal communion would take. Man, Beast, Bird and Fish all grew fearful because this was something new to them and they did not know what to do.

They tried to appease Sun by suggesting that Coyote was of no importance and should be cast out for his betrayal but he would not listen, his retort was that they were all created equally and this is how they should remain.

After what had been hours Coyote awoke and made his way to the mountain unaware of the Sun's fury with him and his followers.

They began to pay their respects to Moon and were surprised to hear Sun bellow back down to them "How dare you treat me like this, lowly dogs."

Coyote looked at Sun slyly and replied.

"Oh cry me a river. You have no power over us. We are moon children now!"

Knowing that he was unable to cry at all, he had only the power to evaporate water, it was Moon who collected the ephemeral mists before they dissipated, then sent them back as rain.

Sun roared with laughter.

'You think you can mock me from your high peaks little dog? We will see who is laughing soon. You should not have angered me!'

Sun had fell into Coyote's trap and his anger caused the mountain to tremble, the surrounding land shook; Man and Beast fell down and trees collapsed.

Coyote began to leap down the mountain as the top of it exploded and the air was filled with poisonous ash and fumes.

Bird began to fly as his perch was toppled and the gases filled the air and Fish swam to the depths to avoid the waves washing him ashore.

Bright orange rocks spewed from the top of the mountain and fiery rivers slowly flowed down the sides boiling and bubbling as they went; consuming all in their path.

Man and Beast ran as swiftly as they could to escape the bubbling flow.

Moon watched all of this and grew fearful that Sun's wrath would destroy all they had created together. She tried to assuage Sun's fury but he would not listen, so intent was he on punishing Coyote for his insolence.

Moon became frustrated and began to weep in sympathy for Man, Beast, Fish and Bird that they were to be punished for the troubles of Coyote. Secretly she also felt strongly for Coyote for he had become a moon child and one of her own.

Her tears met with the fiery mountain and a new battle was waged, the earth cracked, the trees turned black and fell into the chasms or burst into flames and the mountain fell in upon itself as fire and water hissed and boiled.

A great fog obscured the scene for miles around. Man, Beast, Bird, Fish and Coyote (who had managed to escape) all cowered in their hiding places as the land heaved in turmoil.

This great tumult lasted for many days, until at last the skies began to clear. Man called out to Bird and Beast, then sought out Fish and held a high council where they summoned Coyote.

But Coyote laughed at them.

'You all think that you are equal when you are not! Man is weaker than us all, he cannot swim like Fish, he cannot fly like Bird and he cannot run or hunt like Beast and yet Sun and Moon will love him more!'

Man asked Coyote what he meant, but the damage had already been done. Bird returned to his skies, Fish to his rivers and streams and Beast back to his lands. They did not trust Man any longer and eyed each other with suspicion.

Man decided to return to the mountain; the way was hazardous for the land had changed.

It had sharp rocks jutting out of the earth like jagged teeth, no plant life grew and no Beast or Bird could be seen.

Man discovered that the mountain was no more and all that was left was a clear blue lake, the pure water a gift from Moon.

Even today the battle continues, Sun beats down unceasingly throughout the day and Moon refills the lake by night.

Coyote travels the lands alone, shunned by all, but he achieved what he set out to do. All are equal and remain that way.

With the story told Machk stands and makes ready to leave.

'We must not tarry here. Sun and Moon will meet later today and we must get back to the others before the day prematurely darkens. We need to prepare so we can celebrate their union. You must not forget what you have learned today for it needs to be passed to your son one day. Remember to be one with the land and to be friends with the fish, beasts and birds but never trust a coyote. Most importantly do not anger the Gods for it is they who provide for us. Every chieftain must know this for the protection of his tribe.'

'I understand father.'

PART TWO
Flash Fiction

114

BREAKFAST AT TIFFANY'S

BY
QUENTIN COPE

Was she aware of his lingering look, studying her over a coffee cup held unsteadily against a trembling lower lip? She examined the morning newspaper whilst demolishing her second slice of crisp, brown toast; the flitting, fidgeting eyes offering little indication of an interest in anything other than the contents of the daily broadsheet.

Tiffany Wendall had rarely been considered a 'beauty' by those who had met her but to him she was in fact a 'handsome' woman, a successful business manager, a competent mother and a generally enthusiastic lover. Well managed natural blonde hair fell easily down each side of her face, cut expertly to rest evenly on each shoulder. Alice also had blonde hair, but less carefully managed. Alice of course was some years younger than Tiffany, caring less about manageability and more about current fashion.

He put down his cup.
'I'm off now then darling'
'Goodbye dear' she replied without lifting her head ... without making eye contact.
Did she know?

Surely not; he had only decided himself during the early, stomach churning sleepless hours.

He closed the front door quietly, standing motionless next to his car, teeth grinding with the tension of it; the knowledge he would not be coming back.

Tiffany finished the last bite of her toast, a tear falling down her cheek as she pulled the letter from beneath the newspaper, reading it for the thirty fifth time.

"Dear Tiffany, you don't know me but there is something I have to tell you!"

CHRISTMAS PRESENT

BY
KEVIN HORSLEY

"But I don't want to go, I'm not ready yet." Mr Johnson wheezed.

"I haven't had my Christmas dinner yet and my family are due to visit."

The sadness, anger and sheer frustration were palpable to Gabe. It made Gabe feel immense sorrow; the job he had was especially difficult at this time of year.

A nurse came into the room.

"Mr Johnson, your family are here, are you ready to see them?" she asked tenderly.

Gabe smiled, he left knowing that this unexpected gift would be the one they would all appreciate the most.

LIKE CLOCKWORK

BY
KEVIN HORSLEY

With an audible click, it was over. Another working year was done. I sighed with relief.

The lady opposite me at my table glanced up and smiled knowingly as I folded the lid of my laptop down.

I peered from my window and watched the scenery flow by, the speed providing the mirage that the trees had been planted equidistantly apart so each second saw another fly past like the markings on a clock.

It was mid-afternoon. I would be home by dusk. I smile to myself as I realise I am looking forwards whilst travelling backwards and reach into my rucksack for the novel I brought along.

The only thing which was making this journey better was the knowledge that the train was on schedule too.

SNOW BLIND

BY
KEVIN HORSLEY

I am outside having a cigarette, walking around to keep warm and leaving footsteps in the snow. Snow falls heavily around me.

I shiver as I exhale and watch the people milling around in the distance, the heat of the cigarette is a single point of burning intensity against my lips and I know it is nearly done.

I drop it and pull my hood tight and hug myself to warm up a little more, hoping my hands don't get frostbitten.

Taking out my phone from my jacket pocket, I call my wife; Janet. I need to tell her I won't be home in time for the party and that I don't expect to be home until tomorrow. Of all the days for this to happen it had to be her parent's fortieth wedding anniversary.

All I get is static. Frustrated, I type out a text of apology instead. At least this will send when I get a signal. I know in advance that she will not be happy about this, but I am resigned to the fact as, I hope she will accept.

I am tempted to have another smoke but there are so few left and something tells me I will need them later.

The other people are wandering like lost souls. Very few of them have congregated into groups. Most are doing similar activities to me. One or two are huddled on the ground and look like refuse sacks waiting to be collected.

My eyes move across to the train, the long black phallic engine with several carriages attached. It stands motionless on the tracks. If I was not so cold I could appreciate the picturesque Christmas card scene a little more, replete with a robin and skeletal trees dusted with snow.

I climb back aboard and find a steward in the aisle, he directs me back to my seat mumbling that no one knows what has happened but it is being investigated.

Grudgingly I return to my seat and wrap up, I doze off.

I awaken to the commotion of loud thunderclaps.

The steward approaches, he smiles at me.

"It is time." he says simply. Still smiling he continues up the aisle.

I look out of the window and see shimmering doorways appear. As each passenger walks through one, another thunderclap resonates through the air.

Finally I understand. I leave my phone on my seat and exit the train back into the blizzard. I am not surprised to find that there is no chill as I make my way towards the bright outline of a doorway, knowing that I will never return home.

THE PARTY

BY
J.K. SNOWBALL

I was stood in conversation with a group of people I'd never met or couldn't recognise. I didn't know why. I don't even think I knew what the topic was or if I even cared. I remember everyone was having a good time. The dark, clear night sky was filled with stars, dimly lighting the scene, compensating for the absence of the Moon. Fireworks, burst and boomed announcing a celebration of sorts it seemed. A birthday party? A new year's eve party? All I knew was it was a party nonetheless. A garden party, for what event I could not say.

The party guests were dancing, laughing and making polite conversation. The latest pop charts played in the background, a stereo playing so loud you could feel the vibrations ripple through the ground.

My attention was distracted towards a buffet table populated with party foods and cheap drinks. Eating and drinking to my heart's content. Salads, chicken wings, pizza slices, mini sausage rolls Cola, orange juice, beers and wines.

Whatever you desired to eat or drink appeared on that table, as if by magic.

As much as I tried, I could not stop. The desire to consume was simply too much to resist. I eat and I drank till I noticed my belly ballooned to a barrel.

All of a sudden my hands stretched out before me to catch my balance, my vision began to blur and fade. I had no use of my legs and I slowly sank to my failing knees. Then on the ground, I try to reach out for help.

The guests appeared too distracted by conversation and laughter to take notice of me and come to help me. As I lay on the open lawn, powerless to move, I tried to call out but no-one would listen.

A woman I'd never seen or met before ran towards me from the shadows, she clasped my hands in a comforting fashion. My vision faded, then my world went black. I thought that was my end.

I opened my eyes, to find I was in the comfort of my own bed, and at my home, back to my normal size, looking out of my window to see the morning sunrise over the tops of neighbouring houses.

"What did I just experience?" I wondered: perhaps a premonition of my future demise? A link to the demise of a parallel version of myself in a reality not my own? I cannot say. One thing is sure. I was awake: I was alive. I was ready to meet the new day and see what would come.

I learned one lesson from that dream, if I was meant to learn anything at all. It was that you can enjoy the finer things in life, but overindulgence will ruin you and even kill you in time

.

PART THREE
Historical Fiction

An Old Soldier Remembers
By Ange Dunn

Double Cross
By Quentin Cope

The Defeated
By Quentin Cope

Tommy & Benji
By Ethel Stirman

Halcyon Days
Joe Larkin

AN OLD SOLDIER REMEMBERS

BY
ANGE DUNN
Inspiration from Dulce et Decorum Est
by Wilfred Owen

The old man awoke with a start. Yet again he was dragged back to the land of the living, reality harshly disturbing his pitiful slumber. Groggily, he removed the sleep from his eyes, no use to even attempt rest now. He had left that place a long time ago but it had never left him. He had never left him.

He still remembers that night.

The muddy battlefield, he and his fellow soldiers had been ordered into no man's land. Another pointless battle to win the same few miles of land they had previously lost. The smell of gun smoke and death mingled in his nostrils. His boots sank in the land amongst the blood and bones of soldier's remains. The corpse rats who had been happily feasting on his fallen comrades ignored the events around them.

He caught the eye of Jimmy his childhood friend. Jimmy grimaced.

"Better to let the Germans do it and go out a hero than let our chaps call us cowards. Least the wife won't be shamed" Jimmy had called out, a look of resignation on his face

"We are seen as heroes."

The old man had sighed and conceded the point.

127

None of them were heroes though. Every man was cold, tired, muddy and miserable, missing home and feeling as if a part of their humanity was now missing. And scared; they were all scared, jangled nerves on edge as both sides did their best to kill each other.

Before he could respond, the order came. The smell of mouldy hay had filled the air, almost pleasant compared to the horrible stench around them. However, the smell of the colourless gas was one they had learned to dread. Phosgene. Lethal, slow acting and a terrible way to die.

"Gas Gas Gas! " The officer had yelled out. Who was it again? Captain Ramsay? No, Major Saunders. The names fade with time, details merging and becoming confused as his brain slowly gave in to the effects of dementia. Something Jimmy got to escape. Jimmy remains forever young, fixed in the memories and nightmares of those who survived the war.

His death, no matter how torturous, was relatively quick. Quick compared to the slow death the old soldier now faced. Not quick enough to be merciful, the poor victims drowning as their lungs filled with fluid.

The order had been shouted but Jimmy was just too slow to fit the clumsy gas mask that would protect him from the poisonous fumes. Too slow to react. Too slow to realize the order had been given. All they could do was watch in horror as he stumbled and choked. His now corrupted lungs spilling out blood. What was worse was the look on his face, his wide-eyed gaze forever burned into the old man's brain, forever haunting him.

They had flung him onto the wagon with the other victims. He would be dead, or as good as by the time they got him to a medic let alone the hospital. He had been doomed as soon as the toxin had entered his lungs.

The old soldier, the officer and those few who were left standing had paced behind the death wagon. Away from the battle and towards an empty rest. Back to the rats, floods, and lice more lethal at times than the bombs and bullets. It was a macabre march that left them feeling mercifully numb, too exhausted to feel anything but bone-achingly tired. No rest any more, not really. Not then and especially not now.

If the old man had known then what he knew now he would have chosen the gas too. "A coward's way out?" He asked out loud. Nobody replied, and yet they all replied.

Every scream from the dead or dying.

Every bang from the bombs and shells.

Every order, no matter how pointless or dangerous.

He could hear that now as clearly as the day it happened all those years ago. He still heard them all.

Sighing, he turned on his bedside light. It cast a glow over a photograph of his fellow soldiers. A soft glow like a halo. A ray of light from heaven itself. He nodded approvingly at the image it presented. It seemed appropriate. He was the only one left; the last man standing, the one who lived. He knew it would not be much longer before he was joining them. The thought was comforting. Hopefully peace would soon come.

A phrase from one of the war poems he had sought comfort in came to mind. The old Lie: *Dulce et decorum est Pro patria mori.* He mentally translated it. It is sweet and fitting to die for one's country. "A lie, yes. There is no glory in death. Well said, that man," he said softly to himself. He gave a salute to the photograph and went to make himself a cup of tea.

His long day had begun again.

DOUBLE CROSS

BY
QUENTIN COPE

January 6th 1973 – Poltava – Northern Ukraine –
USSR:

Death for sale!

It was an exceptionally cold winter in northern
Ukraine. The early January air temperature
registered minus ten and the wind chill factor
drove it down to twice that on a bleak,
seemingly lifeless Saturday night. Captain
Maksym Borsuk checked his black faced
Poljot. It registered twenty three hundred hours
and four minutes. Any time now!

The snow fell relentlessly on the arrow
straight road between Poltava and Stasi, as it
had done for the past three days, narrowing the
navigable width down to one single track with
ice banks piled up to over a metre on either
side. Captain Borsuk, with three of his troop,
manned a simple red and black striped, single
pole timber barrier, placed across the road
some four miles from the Soviet Military Air
Base at Poltava. It was unusual for a Captain
of the GRU to be attending barricades in the
middle of the night, especially one from the
elite Spetsnaz GRU Tenth Separate Brigade,
but this was an unusual situation. His orders
had been received personally from a very
senior officer without any written back-up or

confirmation. This was not unusual within the secretive world of the Spetsnaz, a unit often called upon to do unusual things in unusual places with some regularly unusual outcomes.

The official looking obstacle had been in place for only ten minutes. He and his troop of eight men waited for one particular vehicle to appear through the near white-out in front of them. It would be coming from the direction of Stasi.

The barrier guards wore the uniforms of standard Russian Airborne Troops (VDV) beneath dark grey greatcoats and heads covered by light blue berets. The four men at the barrier all carried powerful, heavy, rubberized torches and modernised (AKMS) Kalashnikov automatic assault rifles. The remaining five members of the troop hid from view some metres north of the barrier, dug in behind the ice banks.

Straining eyes picked up the glimmer of a single headlight through the continuous snow flurries; then two, then three. The middle one would be a motorcycle escort and the other two would be the following ten ton truck. Maksym considered there could be an escort of some kind behind the truck, either a four wheel drive … or maybe another motorcycle. He spoke into a hand held UHF radio.

'This is the one!' No reply required.

The noise of steel tire studs crunching into the compacted ice became louder and the stabs of light brighter as the small convoy approached. Whatever it consisted of, the plan hadn't changed. It was a simple one, as all good plans were. Kill everyone and take the vehicle.

Junior Sergeant Demichev and Private Ogienko had volunteered to crew the truck that night for the short journey, even though the weather was appalling and there would be a small chance the road to the air base would be blocked with snow drifts. However, for these particular volunteers it was the only way to get through to Air Base A2673 at Poltava, where certain items of illicit cargo would be waiting for them. Demichev was a smuggler; a wealthy smuggler who would be leaving the comforting embrace of the Soviet military in just two years time.

Private Ogienko, his new protégée, would take up the reins of Demichev's business when he eventually left the Air Force. The shipment awaiting their attention tonight consisted of European manufactured hard spirits such as Whiskey and Brandy, cigarettes from the Far East and the biggest money maker of all ... American made, original Blue Jeans. Neither knew details concerning the hardware in the back of the truck. It had been loaded by others, fitted with a tight tarpaulin cover and listed on their work sheet as de-fused munitions. Due to this reason there were not that many volunteers to venture out in a major snow storm and haul a truck load of explosives ... fused or not fused! Demichev felt confident that with the assistance of his collaborators at Poltava, they could unload the munitions and then quickly re-load with his contraband to make it back to their base at Stasi in time for breakfast.

The objective at the moment was to get past what looked like a road block up ahead. Lights could be seen moving back and forth illuminating a red and black barrier pole. Was this a sign they could perhaps go no further or was it just a standard military check by what looked like a bunch of airborne troops with not much else to do but slowly freeze to death on guard duty? It was damn cold inside the cab of the truck, despite the inefficient heater turned up to max, so what it would be like outside in a foot stamping minus twenty was beyond imagination.

The motorcycle crawled up to the barrier, made quite visible by the beams of torches moving casually back and forth across the striped pole supported on two, rusting steel tripods. The motorcycle stopped, as did the KAZ-717 semi trailer behind. The rider dismounted ready to approach the great-coated officer at the barrier, but as he did so, barely heard through the considerable wind noise, a shot was fired. He instinctively turned his head to look back past the truck where he thought the disturbing noise had come from. Straining eyes revealed the morphing shapes of two shadowy figures approaching either side of the truck from the rear.

"What the hell is going on?"

It was, in fact, a final thought; his head grabbed from behind, pulled back sharply and twisted violently to the left. Finally, a stiletto shaft of case hardened blue metal, driven upward beneath his rib cage, ended this particular life. With neck broken and heart ripped apart, the lifeless body of the motorcycle rider fell to the icy roadway. At exactly the same moment, two nine millimetre, hard-nosed bullets ended the promising futures of Junior Sergeant Demichev and Private Ogienko, the remains of which were roughly pulled out of the truck cab and dumped behind the steadily growing ice banks.

The bodies of the two trailing motorcycle escorts and their warm mechanical mounts would quickly follow suit as Captain Borsuk dropped the tailboard and jumped into the canvas topped rear of the truck. He needed to examine its cargo. Four or five pairs of eager hands ripped the canvas cover back behind him. There were, as expected, two sturdy, well manufactured timber ply boxes on the flat bed of the truck. He released the dozen or so snap catches securing the lid of one box to check its contents. Inside, held by tailored anti-vibration brackets and customised mounts sat a black missile shaped object about three metres long and a metre in diameter.

The Spetsnaz Captain pulled his torch downward, to quickly read the light grey Cyrillic scripted code stencilled on the casing of the missile. He grunted in satisfaction. One of his men opened up the other box. The contents were the same. This, so far silent group of highly trained, highly intelligent military specialists were now the proud owners of two Russian manufactured RDS-4, 30 Kiloton nuclear devices. The Captain spoke to the man nearest to him as he vaulted athletically from the back of the truck.

'You … drive the truck. Tell the others to get in under the canvas cover at the back'

'OK Maksym' the soldier replied. First names were always used in Borsuk's unit, regardless of rank.

'Help me with the barrier'

In the yellow glow of the military truck's low grade headlights, the two men threw the pole and two tripods over the snow layered ice banks and with a quick look back to ensure all the men were aboard and out of sight beneath the stiffening canvas cover, they clambered into the cab, pulling the ill fitting doors as tightly closed as possible. The Captain spoke again

'Right … you know where to go. First stop Kremenchuk'

The driver pulled hard on the heater lever, confirming it was working at its highest level, whilst coercing the determinedly stubborn gear lever into first. This was met with some disturbing level of protest from the un-cooperative gearbox. The driver appeared anxious. Captain Borsuk gave him a look, perhaps it was a look of warning or possibly encouragement, but then with a final grating rumble, they were on their way.

~~~~~~

The normal twenty minute drive to the large lock-up store in Kremenchuk took close to an hour. They were now behind time. The door hinges had frozen and required some persuading to open fully. But they needed to get the air force truck off the street and under cover as quickly as possible, and whilst it was still dark. The snow storm had eased and the truck would be easily identifiable sitting out in the middle of the street. Valuable minutes passed; minutes that seemed much longer to Captain Maksym Borsuk as he worked hard with a shovel to move part frozen snow from in front of the troublesome doors. He checked his watch for the twentieth time. They were behind schedule ... and he did not like to be behind schedule.

Using a loading ramp and chain hoist, the nine men transferred the two timber crates weighing around 4,000 Kilos each from the Kaz and into two smaller Kolhida five ton panel trucks. Everyone in the group now knew what was in the timber boxes, remaining silent and thoughtful whilst the re-loading of the two atomic bombs took place. Only Borsuk knew what the cargo would be on this operation before it actually began; the others just followed him. Whatever their mission was, if it was good enough for the Captain, then it was good enough for them. However, that did not mean an amount of nervousness could be sensed amongst the team once they finally knew.

Fully fuelled and eager to get away from the area as quickly as possible, the two trucks edged out of the lock-up into the murky early morning light. The bad weather was a godsend. It had started snowing again and the wind had picked up. There would be few police out on a night like this and any military roadblocks between Kremenchuk and the coastal town of Berdyansk would be passed easily with one simple flash of a Spetsnaz GRU identity card. No one in the military, with even half a brain, would want to take them on. The team, packed inside the two trucks with their sensitive cargo, would need to make up some time on the 330 Kilometre trip to Berdyansk, but Captain Borsuk was confident they would make it without blowing themselves and the southern half of the Ukraine to hell and back.

A route had been mapped out avoiding Dnipro, a town where security was ever high being a centre for Soviet space and defence businesses.

The short detour south would hopefully keep them away from road blocks and not add too much time to their journey. However, arriving on the outskirts of Tokmak the two vehicles became separated in traffic. The situation made Borsuk anxious and he told his driver to pull over at the side of the road. This was a mistake. Being stopped at the side of a road in early morning traffic would attract attention ... and it did.

The tap at the side window of the Kolhida made Borsuk start. He wound down the window. The motor cycle policeman stared the Captain in the face. In the silent visual exchange a question had been asked and Borsuk felt in his camouflage jacket pocket for identity papers. Without a word the policeman took them, studying the picture on the military security pass for a second or two, looking back at the soldier in the truck for a match. It was him alright.

So these guys were the secretive Spetsnaz were they?

He had come up against them once before.

They were, by reputation, not very talkative!

'Why are you stopped in this area Captain? It is not allowed!' said the policeman with some authority.

'We have two trucks ... and it appears we have lost one' advised the Captain with a broad smile, placing the identity documents carefully back inside his jacket, his hand brushing the butt of his Makarov nine millimetre.

The pause was obvious.

What was the policeman thinking? Did he sense danger?

He could be about to make a decision, perhaps a life shortening decision as Captain Borsuk's hand took hold of the pistol. There would be no hesitation.

Without warning the second Kolhida pulled up sharply beside the uniformed figure with a screech of brakes. He turned quickly, left hand dropping to his holstered hand gun; thumb flicking back the security strap.

'Sorry Captain ... I took a wrong turning back there!' shouted the driver across the head of the policeman now sandwiched uncomfortably between the two trucks. He looked up quickly, catching the eye of the Special Forces Captain once more. There would be no more questions. He had suddenly acquired a strong feeling. He would be lucky to get out of this one with his life.

The eyes radiated a silent appeal. The forehead broke out into an uncontrolled dampness. If Borsuk was going to remove the unwanted delay to their urgent journey, now would be the time to do it, with the policeman trapped between the two trucks and shielded from passing traffic. One shot to the head, catch the body before it fell; pull the dead policemen inside the cab of the truck ... and away. It would take only seconds.

Perhaps the fearful policeman knew it.

'There you see ... this is the other truck we were travelling with. Is everything alright now? Can we be on our way?' questioned Borsuk, his tone amiable and unthreatening.

The policeman wiped his sweating brow on the sleeve of his jacket.

'Da!' was the simple grunted reply, his face showing a measure of relief as he turned and walked back to his motorcycle.

'Lets go!' shouted the Captain: 'We've wasted too much time here!'

~~~~~~

Mohamed Shukrani ordered a second cup of coffee. He was nervous, sat at a table, on his own in the coffee shop at the Grand Hotel Excelsior. He cared less the property was regarded as one of the best hotels in the world and certainly the best in Malta, a place he cared for even less. But the Russian had insisted; insisted they meet there, in public.

Colonel General Vladimir Tukanevsky wearing casual slacks and an open necked cotton shirt entered the coffee shop just as Shukrani's coffee arrived.

'I'll have one of those' he announced in perfect English as the waitress smiled in wordless acknowledgement and quickly moved away. The Russian and the Palestinian shook hands. Tukanevsky sat down.

'Are there any cakes?' he asked of his host.

'Is there any bomb? Muttered Shukrani, the comment seemingly directed at no one in particular.

He was not happy to be discussing the theft and transfer of a nuclear device or the movement of large amounts of American Dollars, in public and within possible earshot of others. Although Mohamed Shukrani had taken a circuitous route to get to Malta for the meeting with the Russian General, he couldn't be sure the Israeli Mossad were not on his tail.

'What did you say?' Asked Tukanevsky.

'I said ... is there a bomb, because if there is and it's to be delivered to Cyprus as agreed, we only have the details of the financial transaction to finalise ... and then we are done!'

'Are you in some sort of hurry?'

'Yes ... if you really want to know ... yes, I am in a damn hurry. Insisting we meet here in Malta, one of the most difficult places to get in and out of in the world and meet you in public, in full view of all of the world's not so secret services leaves me more than a little concerned. Maybe you regularly sell the odd nuclear bomb here and there to half the freedom fighters in the world and so this little adventure means nothing to you. However, to me it is the future of my country and the passing on to you of enough money to finance our brave PLO freedom fighters for the next five years!'

Colonel General Vladimir Tukanevsky moved uneasily in his chair weighing up the situation. He didn't like it. This man could be a problem. His coffee arrived and he added a slice of cheesecake with chocolate ice cream to his order gratefully received by the smiling waitress.

'Would you like some?' he asked his table companion before the waitress skipped away.

'No thank you!' It was a clipped, impatient reply.

The Russian took the first sip of his coffee. He was not about to explain to the irate Arab he had men planted all over the coffee shop and covering every hotel entrance and exit. The Arabs were a difficult bunch to deal with and past interactions with some members of the KGB had left two of their number lying in back street gutters with their throats cut. There had never been a shortage of customers for a stolen nuclear device, of whatever size and quality. Terrorist organisations throughout the world were clamouring for one, but most could not afford the price tag and if they could, then the aims of the particular organisation often did not fit well with those of the Soviet Union. Although the Colonel General was part of a group of senior military officers, conspirators looking to take commercial advantage of their position, they also upheld a set of tactical rules whereby their actions would only progress the aims and political philosophies of the Soviet Union as a whole and not damage them.

Sorting out the messy problems in the Middle East by letting off a nuclear bomb would provide an advantage for the Soviets and bring them to the forefront of the table-of-negotiators. It was a win, win situation as seen by the conspirators and to achieve the right end, the Palestinian Liberation Organisation (PLO) had to be today's customer. It was this, or possible all out war in the Middle East and in either situation, people would have to die! There could be no such thing as a conscience in this game; there was too much money involved.

Tukanevsky studied the man fidgeting in front of him. He had a tough reputation and would have preferred someone else to deal with, but this was what he had and now he must make the best of it.

'So, my friend ...' he began: 'let's get down to the bones of the matter. I have a piece of paper in my pocket. On it is written the swift payment codes of three bank accounts. You will need to transfer ten million American dollars to each of these three accounts by midnight tomorrow. When I have confirmation that payment has been received, I will authorise the loading of your 'parcel' on a freighter which waits as we speak at a coastal port on the Sea of Azov'

'I need to know the name of the port'

'No you do not Mr. Shukrani. All you need to know is what I tell you'

The Russian leaned forward. Tension between the two men increased. It was palpable; the locked eyes searching for any point of weakness.

'How can I be sure ...?'

Tukanevsky cut off the Palestinian.

'You can't be sure my friend. In this kind of deal, you can't be sure of anything except this. Whatever you think you can do with your pathetic little band of half starved suicidal teenage militia ... I can do ten times better and five times quicker with my big band of well trained, well equipped and dedicated men. Men that will hunt down you and your fellow rag arsed commanders and cut your damn throats in front of your children ... do you understand?'

Shukrani sat back quickly in his chair. He had gone pale. Perhaps it was the surprise.

Tukanevsky took the first bite of his cheesecake. It was everything he expected it to be.

He looked up. The Arab had nothing to say.

'So, do you want the piece of paper ... or not?'

'Yes' Shukrani murmured.

The General passed it over. The Arab looked as if he was going to open it out and read it.

'No need to read it. Now you can go ... and make damn sure the money is there tomorrow or else the next time we meet there will be no coffee and certainly no offer of a free cheesecake!'

Without another word, Mohamed Shukrani raised himself up from his seat, and with no offer of a handshake he left the coffee shop, making his way through the lobby and out the main entrance of the Grand Hotel Excelsior. It was not a particularly hot day but the Arab sweated profusely. He wiped his forehead with a handkerchief, heart pounding.

The person standing beneath a shading palm tree opposite the entrance to the hotel checked his watch, recording the time his target left the hotel. He would be following him for the rest of the day, as he had done since the PLO commander had arrived on the island.

~~~~~~

The deadline had been set; midday on Sunday, January 7th. They made it to the outskirts of the town with half an hour to spare. Here, the two trucks parted company; one heading east to a lock-up store on Dyumyna Street and the other, containing Captain Borsuk, three men and one crate, toward Yuvleina Street and the gated entrance to the small commercial port of Berdyansk.

Borsuk tapped his driver on the shoulder. The port office located to their left looked busy with people moving in and out avoiding fork lift trucks racing one another from the quayside to the three large warehouses behind the port office. There were half a dozen coastal vessels tied up to the single quay. The one he was looking for was in fact the nearest, a dilapidated looking tramp steamer, the only ship in the port around which there was no activity. The Sea of Azov led into the Black Sea and on through to the Aegean. Borsuk did not know the final destination of a cargo that had so far cost four lives and didn't need to.

He tapped the driver on the arm once more.

'Pull up over there by that old looking boat. I'm going to the port office. If anyone questions you whilst I'm away ... you know what to do'

The driver nodded and Captain Maksym Borsuk slipped out of the vehicle and headed toward the port office.

The counter area was a mass of moving bodies, some obviously bad tempered and most filling in cargo forms, having them stamped, being issued with loading tickets and queuing up for a customs declaration form. A tall uniformed figure behind the counter caught the eye of the Russian Army Officer and pointed to a door on Borsuk's left. He walked through it. The naval officer pushed an envelope into his hand and smiled. That was it. No discussion. Borsuk had what he came for. He quickly opened the envelope. Inside was a single piece of paper with a telephone number written on it. He looked up. The blank faced lieutenant pointed to a small office. It contained a telephone. The thirty second phone call confirmed the cargo could be loaded and then Borsuk's job would be done. As he put the handset down, he was smiling.

On the short walk back to the truck, he raised a hand to his expectant comrades. A forklift waited by the truck. Within minutes, the timber crate was off and carefully secured in cargo hold number three. The boat carried nothing else commercially and was in ballast.

As soon as the one box was loaded, she was to be away.

With doors tightly shut and the three members of his team on board, Borsuk gave the word and the matt grey painted panel truck headed for the port gates.

The whole operation had taken literally minutes. Little or no attention had been paid by anyone to the transfer of the anonymous looking crate containing a 30 Kiloton nuclear bomb. Now, a reward was due - two point seven million US Dollars in used notes. It was where it should be. Maksym had checked; the phone call had confirmed it. That was why he still smiled; one mass killing machine in the bag and one other now under his singular control as a deadly insurance policy. This had been a good day's work.

A hair's breadth!

At dawn on Saturday October 6th, 1973 a coalition of Arab States led by Egypt and Syria invaded Israel. It was the holiest day in the world of Judaism, Yom Kippur and Israel was taken by surprise. Egyptian and Syrian forces crossed previous ceasefire lines in a ruthless and determined move to occupy the Sinai Peninsula in the south and the Golan Heights in the north. Iraq stood poised on the Jordanian border in the east.

In the early hours of Thursday, October 4th, three troops of British SAS, flown up from the Oman, parachuted into Qatar, kidnapped Mohamed Shukrani, personal financial controller for PLO Chairman Yasser Arafat and extracted him to Cyprus by air through Bahrain. He was 'interviewed' by British SIS special operatives on the morning of October 4th showing little resistance and telling his interrogators everything he thought they could safely be aware of. He knew they would need time to check out this new intelligence. He had cleverly avoided indicating any possible moves on Israel, or the actual plan to explode a nuclear device, not more than 250 miles from where the very interrogation itself was taking place. As the first Israeli tank tracks prepared to roll onward toward the Suez Canal the attitude of the Arab conspirator's interrogators changed and within two hours they had the full details.

The vessel carrying the Russian RDS-4 nuclear bomb was quickly located in Limmasol Harbour and captured as it was about to sail. The device, identified as of Soviet stock was immediately disarmed and despatched to the UK on an unmarked C130 Hercules the very same day. The Prime Minister of Israel, Golda Meir had been fully briefed on the known details of the horrific plan to explode a nuclear bomb at sea near the Israeli coastline, as were the Americans and Russians. This intelligence prompted a fierce fight-back by Israeli troops who launched a four day counter-offensive against the Arab invaders. The United Nations brokered a cease fire of sorts on October 22nd but Israel still had work to do encircling the Egyptian Third Army.

Would the Russians step in? There were still questions hanging in the air as to how the Soviets did not know one of their nuclear bombs had gone missing.

It was touch and go with the Americans hovering reluctantly on the brink of full blown military support for Israel.

A second ceasefire was imposed on October 25th, one that finally brought an end to the war.

The Iraqis moved their forces back from the Jordanian border territory in no mood to take on a nation that was now only 40 kilometres from Damascus and 100 kilometres from Cairo.

And so the short but seemingly decisive Yom Kippur war would end. But to the Arabs this was much less a war than a battle; the war itself was to continue and a bitter and more violent era of Middle East terrorism would begin. The big question of the twenty first century is 'when will it ever end?'

THE DEFEATED

BY
QUENTIN COPE

January 25th 1959 – Jebel Akhdar – The Oman Interior.

It was dark and cold sitting on the damp, clay floor within the confines of the half destroyed hut on the edge of Bani Habib village. This was Jebel Akhdar, a high plateau reaching to 10,000 feet on the edge of Oman's Al Hajar mountain range. The temperature, at minus three degrees centigrade, was low enough for the thirty one year old Englishman sitting huddled in the corner of the dilapidated shelter. He wore a British Army greatcoat bearing the blackened shoulder pips of a Captain and stood out from the others. Opposite him, clutching Martini rifles and putting together the required items to light a fire were the Imam of Awabi, Sulayman bin Abdulla and his brother, Tammam bin Abdulla. They were both in their late forties with birth dates somewhere between 1908 and 1912, depending upon which calendar you preferred to consult, but however old they both really were, they were fit, hard mountain fighters and they looked the part. Along with their military ally, Aasif bin Hashem, they were all wanted men, dead or alive and had been on the Sultan of Oman's list for some years.

The natural fortress of Jebel Akhdar had protected them for all that time, but the chill, relentless wind cutting across the Jebel that night, would bring with it betrayal, death and unexpected disaster. The sparks of a fire now moved to a flame as Tammam bin Abdulla carefully placed small, dried kindling sticks over the smouldering sun burnt grass. Within minutes, the fire had begun to roar, fed by two men who had entered the hut with armfuls of dried acacia branches. Immediately a dozen other fires blazed away surrounding the hut with several tribal fighters gathered around each; mostly chatting loudly or smoking small copper lined pipes drinking in the welcome warmth, leaning on their long barrelled Martini-Henry rifles, the weapon of choice in the Oman peninsular.

Small arms fire could be heard in the distance along with the odd flat, low register rumble of 81mm mortars. There was much activity in the north, as there had been for most of the day. The British 'A' Squadron SAS was pushing hard into the Imam's defences at Hajar and Aqabat al Dhafar. It was decision time. One of the donkey men loyal to the Imam and his cause had been at the British briefing the day before. Something serious was about to happen, but not the way the briefing Army Major had explained it. The Sultan of Oman and his British friends were determined to remove the Imam one way or another and end his rightful claim to being the religious and political leader of the Oman interior. This was not about political power, it was about money and that money was ripe to rise up out of the ground in the form of oil; a black sticky currency desperately needed by a still colonial minded Britain that sent mercenaries and the finest of British Special Forces to solve what was essentially a problem of history and tribal rights. The British were expert at supporting despotic regimes in third world countries. Their leaders were usually quite ruthless, had little or no social conscience and were sometimes proven to be completely mad, but the main thing was to make sure they were compliant. The Sultan of Oman filled all of these requirements admirably. The Imam spoke first.

'Well Maxwell my friend' what is your advice now?'

'I have a feeling we are somewhere in between 'a rock and a hard place … as our American cousins would put it'

Captain Maxwell Armstrong, British military advisor, was seconded as a negotiator between the Imam, the Sultan's representatives and the Commander of the British SAS forces in the Oman. He had been with the Imam and his tribal army for over a year now and had got to know the man well. He had used his time on the Jebel to learn Arabic. He had been summoned by the Sultan and should have been off Jebel Akhdar two days ago. He knew nothing of what was to shortly happen on the plateau. He was not party to high level military briefings, but he did know by the change of tactics over the past three days, that something was about to happen and tonight was probably the night. The aerial campaign by British Lancaster bombers and Venom jets had suddenly stopped and now there were literally hourly probes by the SAS in the north. The Imam had around fifteen hundred brave mountain fighters loyal to him on the Jebel and it would be up to him to decide whether or not these valuable lives should be sacrificed or spared in any ensuing battle. Tammam, the Imam's younger brother spoke.

'We should stand and fight ... look at the damage we have done to the stupid Nasrani already. If we attack now in the north, we stand a chance of defeating them'

'Chai' arrived and the men in the hut took a glass each of the over sugared black tea and began to drink.

There was silence for a minute or two. The Imam, although tired, looked equally relaxed as he looked toward his English friend for a response. Maxwell simply shook his head. The Imam finally spoke.

'My brothers ... my heart is heavy and sad but I must consider the lives of all our brave followers who will get little or no mercy from the devilish agents of the Sultan. We will finish our tea and then move to Sharqiyah, where we have friends who will look after us and our brave fighters can disperse toward the Gulf coast, God willing'

Everyone in the hut remained silent; if this was the will of the Imam then it would not be questioned. Tammam was about to say something, but held back as he got up from his cross legged position and moved outside to organise the body guard of over eighty battle hardened fighters.

'Will you be coming with us Maxwell?' the Imam asked in a low, slightly emotional voice.

'No my old friend, that is not possible. I fear that something will be happening here tonight and I think you should leave as quickly as possible. I will stay here and if all is well in the morning, I will move north to meet up with the Trucial Oman Scouts at their Rustaq camp'

The Imam raised himself as did the English Captain. They hugged together for a long moment, a sign of great affection between two men from such differing backgrounds and cultures. Both picked up their rifles and ammunition bandoliers and left the hut. A great shout went up from the assembled tribesmen as they shot the blackened clouds with endless rounds of ammunition. Finally all was silent. The Imam raised his arms, turned to look back at Maxwell and then disappeared out of the ring of light provided by the still burning fires and into the misty shadows of the night, followed silently by his shabby looking band of rebel fighters.

~~~~~~

The commander of 'D' Squadron SAS was facing a dilemma in his attempt to lead his troops on what would be a most difficult ten thousand foot climb up to the top of Jebel Akhdar in broad daylight. Unfortunately it was not broad daylight. It was three o'clock in the morning and his troops were fading fast as they reached the operationally coded 'Causeway' … a mountain crest about one third of the way up to the top of the Jebel itself. He had to do something or his troops would not reach the plateau by daybreak. Each soldier carried a Bergen rucksack weighing nearly ninety pounds. He made the decision and ordered his men to remove the ammunition and grenades and then stash the rucksacks on the ridge. If they survived the night, they could come back later for clothes, canteens and food rations. If they didn't, then they wouldn't need them. The part trek and part climb continued with no rest.

When daylight finally came, 'D' Squadron and 'A' Squadron SAS were on the plateau. They were exhausted. There was no expected resistance, in fact the only sign of what could be called 'the enemy' was a small band of about twenty Bani Riyam tribesmen who were quite happy to 'surrender' if that was what the white, Christian soldiers ….   the 'Nasrani'… wanted. There was no sign of the Imam Sulayman bin Abdulla or his brother Tammam bin Abdulla. There was also no sign of Aasif bin Hashem the leader of over two thousand 'rebel' fighters …. or the very fighters themselves. The so called 'rebellion' was over. After four long years, Jebel Akhdar had been taken. The London Times described the operation undertaken by the SAS on that dark day January 25th, 1959 as 'a brilliant example of economy in the use of force'. Maxwell Armstrong knew better.

TOMMY AND BENJI

BY
ETHEL STIRMAN

"Hey up, Benji, what's the matter with ye lad?" Tommy tugged harder on the bridle but the pit pony stubbornly refused to budge. He wouldn't even take the strain to pull the tub laden with timber props in bye through the tailgate to the coal face. Puzzled, Tommy tried a different tack, speaking quietly to his friend, gently stroking the soft spot behind his ear; this usually worked to move the pony on.

Still Benji refused to move. Tommy was stumped. It wasn't like the pony which usually took little persuasion to pull the timber props in bye. There would be hell to pay when Tadger Brown, the deputy, got to hear of it. Tommy had been so proud to be given the chance to lead his own pony; he was the youngest timber in the pit and liked to make sure the other lads knew it too.

"Howay Tommy lad, get that hoss outa my way, will ye? They're waiting on me to get the face away. I'm already running late and there'll be ructions on if I don't make the face before Tadger finishes giving the jobs out."

Stan Serrill was an electrician who lived in the same street as Tommy and Tommy was well aware that he was just as likely to get a clout off Stan if he held him up any further.

"Sorry Mr. Serrill but it's Benji: he's refusing to enter the tailgate. I don't know what's wrong but something's spooked him that's for sure."

Any other time, Stan might have stopped to consider the pony's odd behaviour, but he was late because he'd been out on the beer the night before, and had already had a warning because it wasn't the first time it had happened. In fact, since his Susie had finally got fed up with his drinking and left him, it had become somewhat of a regular occurrence.

"Well I can't help that, Tommy, now squidge 'ower and let me through."

Tommy pushed the pony up tight against the wall allowing Stan to squeeze past and hurry on towards the coal face.

All of a sudden, Benji began to toss his head, ears flattened back, eyes rolling wildly, tearing the bridle from young Tommy's grasp.

There was a low rumbling sound, then sharp cracks as props supporting the tailgate snapped clean in two. Huge clouds of dust spewed forth as great blocks of stone broke free from the roof, crashing down and completely blocking the way. The pony screamed in fear, crashing into Tommy, flinging him back against the wall, banging his head and leaving him unconscious in the absolute blackness.

As Tommy gradually came to, he could feel the cold steel of the rails against his legs. He had no way of knowing how long he had been out for. It might have been minutes or it could have been hours. It couldn't have been too long, he thought, because he was aware of the light still shining dimly from his cap lamp.

By this weak light he could see the

devastation that surrounded him. A whole section of roof had fallen in the tailgate ahead and the way was totally blocked. Dust still made it difficult to see clearly and to breathe. He struggled to sit up; something was pinning his legs but it didn't feel hard or solid but warm and soft. It was Benji; the pony had taken the brunt of the fall, shielding Tommy from the avalanche of rock from above.

Tommy was struck by dread for his faithful friend but soon realised that, Benji, far from being dead, was still breathing above him. Gently, he slid his hand along the pony's neck until he found the soft spot behind Benji's ear and stroked him gently, being rewarded with a soft snort in reply.

"Don't worry bonny lad, they'll soon get us out of here."

Although Tommy had heard many horror stories of cave-ins down the pit, he knew that others had miraculously survived. He was sure that the deputy on the coalface would have contacted the surface to report the rock fall and that the rescue team would already be on its way to dig him out. He was lucky that there was space around him; the fall had been much worse further up the tailgate. Thank goodness Benji had refused to enter. He must have sensed something was wrong with the way ahead and ultimately had saved Tommy's life.

Tommy shone his lamp towards the tailgate opening but the light reflected back from a solid wall of stone.

Suddenly Tommy remembered Stan Serrill. Had he made it through to the face before the fall or was he too trapped helplessly longing for rescue.

Although fear constricted his throat, Tommy worked some saliva into his dust-choked mouth and called out into the dark.

"Stan!"

No answer.

"Stan! Are ye there? Are ye alright, Stan?"

All Tommy could hear was his own heart thundering in his ears.

"Stan! Stan, c'mon man, answer me!"

"Aye, Tommy, I'm here lad."

Relief washed over Tommy. Stan was alive. He was not alone.

"Are ye alright, Stan?"

"I'm fine, Tommy, but it looks like we might be stuck here for a while, son. Can you reach your water bottle, Tommy? Yer've gotta take a drink, son, but not too much now; yer've gotta make it last."

"Okay, Stan, ee I've never been so glad to another voice,"

"Yer'll be fine, Tommy. Now take a drink then rest. Remember your training: try to stay awake; don't let the gas get to ye. Rest easy; save your strength bonny lad; we don't know how long they'll take to reach us."

Tommy took a mouthful of his precious water but couldn't resist cupping his hand to give a little to Benji. "Here you go fella. It's not much but I daresay your throat's just as dry as mine."

Benji whinnied his thanks and nuzzled Tommy's hand. Tommy switched off his cap lamp to save the battery for later. Together, boy and pony, were glad of each other as they settled down to wait for the pit rescue team to arrive.

Gradually Tommy drifted into a deep sleep as the darkness and silence closed around him. As he slept, he dreamt of home: the cosy colliery house where he lived with his mother and father, two brothers and a sister, all older than him. He was the baby of the family, a little spoiled perhaps but loved dearly by them all.

He was sitting in his father's chair by the range fire. It was already dark outside and his mother sat opposite him in a rocking chair, quietly knitting and humming a restful tune. The soft clacking of her needles and the warmth of the fire made him drowsy. His mother looked up, a comforting smile gracing her lips. She leant forward towards him, "Tommy! Tommy! Stir yerself son, it's time for bed."

Tommy could hear her but was finding it difficult to rouse himself.

"Aye Ma, in a minute."

He thought he could hear a banging. Was there someone at the door? What could they want at this hour?

Clang! Clang! Clang! Tommy realised the noise resonated from under him. It was travelling along the rails beneath his trapped legs.

Clang! Clang! Clang! There it was again.

Tommy shook his head, regaining consciousness. He scrabbled around looking for something, anything to answer the banging. His hand at last closed around a loose stone. He banged three times on the iron rail and was overjoyed when almost immediately he received three answering clangs.

His mind turned to Stan trapped further down the tailgate.

"Stan! Stan! Did you hear that? They've found us, Stan, they'll soon have us out!"

But no reply came from the trapped man.

Tommy ran his hand gently over Benji's neck. The pony lay still but he could feel his heart still beating rhythmically under his hand.

Turning on his cap lamp, he focussed its weak beam onto the wall of stone behind him. At last he could see the stone begin to give; splinters of rock breaking off, cascading down towards the floor. A gap appeared and he could feel the rush of clean air as the rescue team broke through.

A bright beam of light pierced the darkness and Tommy felt relief flood through him as a deep voice rang out.

"Hello is anyone there?"

"Aye, it's me Tommy Wainright."

"Thank God you've found me."

"Are you alright, lad? Are you hurt?"

"I'm okay, but my legs are trapped under my pony. He took the worst of it when the roof came down. He's not dead but I'm worried he might be hurt bad."

The banging began again in earnest and soon the hole was big enough to see the rescuer's face peering through at him. Tommy didn't know whether to laugh or cry.

"You've gotta hurry cos Stan Sterrill is buried further up the tailgate and now he's not answering me."

"Alright lad we'll soon be through. Just you hang in there and try to stay calm."

The hole grew bigger until at last the men could make their way through. They soon had most of the debris cleared off the pony and Tommy was pulled free from beneath the animal's flank. Once freed, Tommy was delighted to see Benji struggle to his feet, his soft muzzle seeking the comfort of Tommy's hand. Tommy felt in his pocket for the carrot he always kept there for the end of shift and fed it gratefully to his friend.

"Do you know what?" he said to the rescuer: "That pony saved my life."

"Aye he certainly took the main force of the fall."

"No, not just that. He wouldn't go down the tailgate. He must have sensed the roof was going to fall and refused to go on."

"I've worked on this job too long to be amazed at anything that can happen down a pit. I reckon you've both had a lucky escape. Now we need to push on and try to get to your marra. Stan did you say his name was?"

"Aye it is. I hope he's holding on in there."

One of the rescue team gave Tommy a quick check over; they were all well trained in first aid, and then escorted him to the shaft bottom to get the cage to the surface. Another of the team would see Benji safely back to his stall in the underground stable. Behind them, Tommy could hear the banging start up again as the rescue team began to clear the next section of the fall.

At the surface, Tommy's family and friends

waited anxiously. They had gathered there several hours ago, as soon as the pit buzzer had sounded to let the mining community know there had been a bad accident down the mine. All those with men on shift had immediately made their way to the pit head to wait for news.

Gradually most of the men had come to the surface and made their way home with their relieved families, leaving only Tommy's family and friends to their lonely vigil. Later they were joined by Susie Serrill who hadn't been able to stay away when she got word of the plight of her estranged husband.

As Tommy emerged from the lamp cabin into the open air, the Wainrights surged forward to gather him into their waiting arms. But there would be no such comfort for Stan Serrill.

Later, Tommy learned that the roof fall had been much worse further up the tailgate and Stan had almost certainly been killed outright when the tons of stone fell down on him. Despite this, Tommy was certain that Stan had been there with him during his terrifying ordeal. His encouraging voice had kept him positive; his very presence giving him comfort and hope in his hour of need.

Whenever Tommy and Benji entered the tailgate, pulling their tub laden with timbers, he remembered Stan and a smile crossed his face.

HALCYON DAYS

BY
JOE LARKIN

I finally plucked up the courage to take hold of Dorothy Malone's hand for the first time. From beneath the brim of her hat, Dorothy revealed a tender smile, silently acknowledging our joined hands.

"Dear God!" I thought "It's taken me ages to pluck up the courage!"

Elation surged through me and, at the same time, disbelief. Should I pinch myself? I was closer to my beautiful Dot than at any other time in our courtship.

I strolled through the best summer of my whole life, the late afternoon sun kissing the two of us as it slowly descended behind the distant hills. Along the way, we kept looking at each other intensely, our eyes engaging in intimate conversation. We just knew ... !

I gently steered Dorothy toward the steps that led down to the beach; at the bottom, we took off our shoes and walked barefoot on the sand to the water's edge.

We looked at each other and a flash of childish madness came upon us both, causing me to roll up my trouser-legs, whilst Dorothy raised her skirt hem to tie a knot in it just below her knees. Laughing and giggling, we skipped backwards and forwards in the cold exhilarating sea until we'd become accustomed to the tingling sensation lapping over our feet.

After a few minutes, our playful giddiness subsided and once again, holding hands, we continued to walk along the beach. In this idyllic setting, we found ourselves completely alone.

Turning close into my lovely Dot, I held her by the waist, and gazed into her eyes; those lustrous eyes which acknowledged our mutual desire to kiss for the first time.

All day, in my head I'd practiced this moment and now I counted (one ... two ... three), dipping my head slightly to kiss her sweet lips.

~~~~~~

"Stand to ... Stand to ... Stand to, you lazy bastards. Hands off yer cocks and pull up yer socks!"

Corporal Farrar swiftly followed through with a heavy kick to the soles of our hob nailed ammo boots (regulation issue), and continued down the trench barking out the first order of the day with filthy language, kicking anybody who still hadn't shown signs of waking up.

Farrar was one of the crudest blokes I'd ever met, but he was a bloody good soldier with five Hun kills to his name since September; one of them 'hand-to-hand.'

The crack of dawn was still two hours in front. Harry and I resembled dishevelled scratchy old men, arthritically rolling out from underneath our blankets and an additional improvised blanket of two greatcoats buttoned together. The extra warmth this ingenious coupling provided immediately left our-lice infested bodies.

After rapidly completing basic ablutions with cold water and a little piece of shared carbolic soap we alerted our minds to the task ahead, and got busy putting our clobber and fighting kit on, which helped shake off the early morning-shivers and create a little bit of self-generated heat.

With the rest of the battalion we took our place next to the fire-step. Standing at ease, facing the trench wall, I glumly considered our privations: lack of regular sleep, lack of good hot scoff, a much needed hot bath to delouse the body and a clean uniform.

Having 'chats' (lice) was like a nagging toothache and something you wouldn't wish on your worst enemy. Any opportunity to take off our shirts we did, and like little old tailors we'd sit crossed legged 'chatting', killing the little buggers by running lit candles down the inside seams.

The chats would pop like fire crackers. Shaking off your shirt gave instant relief. But, this was short lived as the female eggs were hard to get to most of the time and bloody impossible to get rid of completely.

I was about to continue with this pitiful train of thought when I looked above the parapet, transfixed at how a cold and ungodly hour such as this could produce the beginning of a day that looked so beautiful with a huge full moon off to my left and all around the backdrop of a star-filled, dark blue to black firmament. Standing stock-still I craned my neck heavenwards and, with eyes as big as saucers, stared open-mouthed.

I thought to myself "Wondrous ... bloody wondrous!"

I felt a sharp dig in my right arm.

"Flipping heck, Harry! What was that for?"

"Stop ruddy daydreaming. Walt! It's time for 'Morning Hate.' Get yourself ready!"

Of all the monotonous routines we played out every day, 'Morning Hate' was, in my opinion, the most futile and bloody dangerous, dreamt up by the brass hats I have no doubt. It was meant to let the enemy know we were on the ball, and still here (much to our displeasure), by firing a hellish load of lead at their front line. But what did I know as a buckshee Private? Ours not to reason why...

The Company Adjutant, Captain Bickerstaff, (a real pukka gent if there ever was one) gave the initial order to commence, handing over to Serjeant Johnson to deliver the words of command to Z Company. With rifles loaded and bayonets fixed, we mounted the fire-step in unison. For a couple of seconds we waited with our heads just below the parapet. Serjeant Johnson then gave the order to engage the enemy with rapid fire.

Simultaneous orders were given in the other three rifle companies and for the next forty-five minutes, 713 able-bodied men of the 2nd Battalion maintained a constant fusillade of rounds at the enemy trenches. In support were two Vickers machine guns laying down 500 to 600 rounds of ammunition per minute.

Needless to say, the Germans didn't just sit there! They threw back a ton of lead in our direction.

When the order to cease fire came, my hands trembled for an age, ears ringing and my face (grimy most days) was even dirtier from the Stand to, Stinking Cordite Party, we'd been so cordially invited to. The aftermath of every 'Stand to' was a minimum of one or two of our blokes dead and a handful suffering bullet or shrapnel wounds to the head or upper body.

To me, it was really no consolation knowing that Fritz had suffered the same, if not worse. This was sheer attrition and all of us on both sides were on borrowed time. But before destiny came knocking, it was time for our rum ration.

This particularly glorious sunny morning, we were served up a breakfast we rarely saw; fresh bread, butter and fried bacon brought up in containers from behind our lines! Something fishy was brewing, and it wasn't the Serjeant Major's tea (which was always a decent brew with real milk and sugar!). Must be a catch…

~~~~~~

Harry Beckinsale and I have been best pals since we were nippers. Harry lived in a big house on Caledonia Road and I lived in a two-up two-down in Woodbine Square, less than half a mile away. At five years of age we became inseparable, and have remained so.

My name is Walter Dixon, and this is our story.

We were born in March 1895 and neither of us had any brothers or sisters. So, we decided to become 'brothers' at the tender age of ten on one summer afternoon in Tipton Woods. After spending all day climbing the biggest trees and nicking blackbird and song thrush eggs, plus (according to Harry) one dubious 'sparrow-hawk' egg. (sparrowhawk? No way, Harry!)

We sat down by the little beck in the top right-hand corner of the woods, and winced our way through the sourest crab-apples yet.

It was during this feast that Harry stuck his hand in his trouser pocket and took out his treasured bone-handled penknife, pulled the shiny two-and-half-inch blade out of its case and scraped a few scabs off his apple, then handed it to me to do likewise.

After we'd devoured half a dozen apples between us (guaranteeing belly ache later, but who cares?) Harry looked at me, straight-faced and spoke seriously.

"Walt, you I and should become blood brothers; being blood brothers will make it real. Agreed?"

I couldn't disagree; I just knew what it meant... pain! Not that I was 'windy' mind you (not in front of my best pal at least). Before I could say anything, Harry dramatically sliced the blade across his thumb; crimson red blood immediately dribbled from the cut.

It was my turn, but I couldn't do it to myself. Harry guessed that was the case (he knew me better than I gave him credit for), so before I could think of chickening out, he grabbed my wrist, and quick as a flash deftly butchered me with no time to grimace or even say "ouch!"

I looked at him, wide-eyed and tight-lipped, then looked at my bloodied thumb, awkwardly sticking upright as if I'd given this ancient ceremony the blooming thumbs-up!

Harry, sounding like d'Artagnan, made the grandest speech I'd heard in my short life, binding both of us together, vowing mutual loyalty, trust, and other good lines I fail to remember due to the initiation's shock effect upon me.

Whenever we reminisced about our 'blood pact,' we always cracked up laughing at my reaction ... Brothers.

My father (a regular soldier) was shipped to South Africa in 1898 to take part in the Second Boer War when I was only three, leaving me with just a vague memory of him in uniform, a broad smile on his face, holding me aloft and kissing my forehead whilst my dear mother sobbed quietly at the kitchen table. Then he was gone, never to return; shot dead by a Boer sniper and laid to rest in a foreign field called Ladysmith.

For a long time I couldn't remember anything about him, although I never forgot his gentle eyes and his smile.

Mother appeared stoic, but sometimes I heard her weeping through the thin walls. I was aware of her grief, but never wanted to share it. She worked hard, taking in commercial laundry from businesses in Jubilee Street and also did the twilight shift, weaving worsted fabric at the

Crompton & Slater Woollen Mill, while our neighbour Mrs Pearson looked after me.

Mother's endeavours went a long way to supplement her Army Widows War Pension and, God bless her, she kept our heads above water.

Mother was a devout Roman Catholic and every Sunday we attended Mass. After Mass she lit a candle and prayed for her husband's soul. We thoroughly enjoyed each other's company on Sundays, and the thrill of riding the new-fangled motorbus into town and back was enough to keep me moderately still for an hour in church.

I met Harry on our first day at Alma Primary School. That morning, stern tight-lipped teachers marched into the playground, shouting children's names and proceeded to herd us into columns of new infant classes, ordering, laying firm hands on little shoulders and pushing us to our respective lines, creating urgency, panic and confusion amongst the many startled faces; daunting to say the least, with several of the kids shedding tears and the rest of us suffering from acute trepidation.

The exception was Harry, who stood in the middle of all this anxiety with a genuine grin upon his face. He was different; tall for his age, a rangy physique, topped off with a shock of straw blonde hair and piercing blue eyes, exuding a confidence that none of us other kids had. From the very beginning we bonded, as close as if we were identical twins.

Our early school years went joyously by in a blur. Both of us had achieved good marks in our reading, writing and arithmetic tests, allowing us to be enrolled at the new Marlborough Elementary School for Boys and benefiting from what was considered at the time higher education and an additional five years in school.

Thankfully Mother had the blessing of only two mouths to feed, and enough regular income (low as it was) to diligently salt away small amounts of money to pay towards my extra years at school. Harry's parents fared somewhat better, as Mr Beckinsale was a senior clerk at the Priestley Bridge Forge (steel foundry) on the outskirts of town.

Mr and Mrs Beckinsale were Wesleyan Methodists and like my mother took their faith seriously enough to ensure Harry toed the line when it came to church and Sunday school attendance, much to his chagrin. His parents were very kind towards me, Mr Beckinsale especially so. He always went out of his way to encourage me in my schoolwork, sport, life-lessons, everything!

Over the years his support meant an awful lot to me.

"Walter my lad, you've got a good head on your shoulders, you're a credit to your mother, and father, God rest his soul. Keep up the good work son, you won't regret it."

Whenever he called me son (even if it was just his turn of phrase) I glowed inside, a right good feeling; special like.

Teasingly, Harry always prodded me whenever his dad called me son, telling me I was his 'gooseberry-bush' brother. Mr

Beckinsale had a full set of Chambers Encyclopaedias and would loan me a volume whenever I wished (which was always!).

Every Saturday during the football season he would take Harry and me to watch Town play in the Second Division. He treated me equally alongside Harry. Mr Beckinsale was a good man, one of the best.

We absolutely loved football and nearly every day during the summer holidays we kicked Harry's leather ball around the streets and nearby park for all it was worth. On Sunday afternoons if I wasn't with my mother I was in paradise, whanging the football against the cobblers gable wall by myself.

Nearby Harry sweated sullenly for an hour in the Methodist church hall, along with his co-religionists learning word verbatim psalms, proverbs and reading out loud tracts of the Bible. A couple of hymns always indicated the end of lessons. On Harry's instruction (or suffer a fate worse than death) I had to be waiting on the grass verge outside the hall when the doors flung open.

A sudden surge of noisy kids would come flying out with Harry in front and a face like thunder. I couldn't stop myself from laughing, immediately passing him the ball, in turn he would run at it and give it an almighty toe-ender, as high into the air as possible. Within seconds his usual jovial disposition had returned; a big silly grin on his face and all was well in our world once more.

In the July of 1910 aged fifteen Harry and I finally left school, armed with our Higher

School Certificates. We both felt excited for the future, but at the same time I was somewhat reticent, a slight fear of stepping forward into a world we'd fortunately avoided, whilst many of our contemporaries from poorer families had had no choice but to eke out a living for the last three years.

With influence and support from his father, Harry started work in the September as a boy clerk at Priestley's.

I got a position as a solicitor's junior runner with the firm Cooper, Franks and Ainsworth in Jubilee Street. Mother had kept their office laundry clean for several years and proudly spoke of me to Mr Cooper whenever she had the opportunity, and especially of my time at Marlborough Elementary, always mentioning my progress and achievements.

She was a very persistent woman. On the day I received the good news of obtaining gainful employment, her abiding advice was, "Son, you're in the real world now. Never let it be said your mother bred a shirker." Mother's work ethic was legendary.

Leaving the relative safety of school and embarking on my journey into the big wide world was daunting to say the least. Not until I was eighteen did I feel able to cope with this all-consuming, tricky environment.

I escaped whenever I could, playing left full back for Albion Athletic in the local football league on a Saturday afternoon. Or, when I was totally engrossed in the pink pages of the Union Jack weekly, following the exploits of Sexton Blake successfully solving the most dastardly and ingenious cases of criminality. Harry, on the other hand, took to everything like a duck to water.

Now standing a good three inches taller than me (and two inches on his dad), he unconsciously commanded respect from people, far beyond what his youth would ordinarily allow. At work he mastered his duties quickly and was keen to learn, never ceasing to ask his supervisor and elder colleagues questions to help him improve.

Harry was extremely conscientious and this quality was recognised early on by the General Manager, who took a personal interest in his development.

On his eighteenth birthday Harry was elevated to the position of substantive clerk and it looked more than likely in the coming years he would continue to make impressive progress, surpassing his father into senior management and the boardroom. Harry clearly had ambitions, not in any way greedily or aggressively; he was just naturally blessed with self-assurance. Harry truly loved his father and vice versa, but they were as different as chalk and cheese.

In my work I wasn't doing too badly either. I'd been diligently working at Cooper Franks and Ainsworth for three years and learnt a great deal. I'd become more confident in my knowledge of civil and criminal law and gained a growing respect from the partners and other staff. I'd recently been promoted to runner (with a surprisingly decent wage rise), and my duties increased considerably.

I was now trusted to pick up and deliver confidential legal documents at other law firms, filing important papers at the town courts and on occasion travelling further afield. I enjoyed serving subpoenas the most, feeling very 'legal' handing over the document to the person concerned. A natural ability to listen, pay attention and an eye for detail enabled me to put my foot in the door of the legal profession.

My intention was to advance to legal clerk in the next three years and maybe achieve the dizzy height of solicitor someday! The day of my promotion I rushed home to tell my mother the good news. She was over the moon. That very evening I also told Mr Beckinsale and he was genuinely thrilled for me, full of praise and warmth as always.

A week later when I visited Harry at his home, Mr Beckinsale presented me with a leather-bound 2nd edition volume of the Digest of the Law of England. It must have cost a small fortune. I was absolutely overwhelmed.

~~~~~~

The two of us entered 1913 heady with optimism for our future. Harry got off to a cracking good start. At church he was introduced to a very pretty young lady, tall and elegant for her age, looking every inch the Gibson Girl (the fetching fashion of the day). Her name was Eleanor Lucinda Fergusson the seventeen-year-old daughter of the newly appointed Methodist Minister, Reverend Robert. He was not the usual hellfire and brimstone type of preacher, but measured, quietly spoken, with a gentle smile and contemplative air; attributes that endeared him to all. The Reverend was a widower, tragically losing his wife to typhoid fever early on in their marriage. Harry was smitten. Whenever he was in Lucy's presence he looked just like a Golden Labrador in a trance, obediently sitting in front of his mistress. Needless to say, he wasn't so quick to exit the church on Sundays anymore and most unusually he even started to volunteer his services to the church ministry.

It was a picture to witness, this rapid metamorphosis, and poking fun at him was my rich reward. As usual he took it in his stride, cool as a cucumber, always a slight grin on his face.

Harry was allowed to escort Lucy to the recently opened Taylors Tea Rooms in Jubilee Street on Saturday afternoons. He was also permitted to 'walk out' with her on a Sunday afternoon, in Royal Victoria Park, but wasn't allowed to take her to the Electric Palace, which showed the new and amazing animated pictures imported from America. I can only suspect the reason was that the theatre lights were dimmed whilst the programme was shown.

For a cleric Reverend Robert had a refreshingly liberal approach to life but he also knew that unfounded gossip in a close-knit parish was gossip all the same.

~~~~~~

Harry and I flew through 1913 like racing pigeons and it seemed to us people in general had a sense of this strange speeding up of time. And then, as a fast train eventually reaches its destination, it begins to slow down; wheels screeching, bringing the mighty force to a permanent halt. All the carriage passengers quickly disembark onto the platform, doors slamming shut and finally the engine falls silent … hissing steam spent. Some of us knew what was happening in Europe; the continuous sabre-rattling of empires and their jostling for supremacy. We weren't stupid, far from it. Reading between the lines a storm was looming, no matter how the politicians tried to deny it. We just knew.

Our dreams changed as the year drew on and any prospect of a settled life, with the ability to pursue our destinies, seemed less tangible. As our small world lurched towards uncertainty Harry and I made a joint decision to enlist in the army prior to what we thought was the inevitable onset of war. This was the guarantee we could stay together, so on Monday 5th January 1914 we had a perfunctory medical examination and declared fit and healthy to carry out military service.

We recited our oath of allegiance to King and country, signed our attestation forms, took the King's shilling and enlisted as regular infantry soldiers in the Koylis (King's Own Yorkshire Light Infantry). Within the week we'd resigned our positions at work and bade farewell to all the people we loved. Our mothers were inconsolable. Mr Beckinsale endeavoured to be calm and matter-of-fact, but I could tell he was utterly devastated; eyes full and bottom lip quivering imperceptibly. Lucy and Harry had made a pact to wait for each other. Placing a small photograph of herself in Harry's breast pocket, she kissed him and with tears streaming down her cheeks, turned on her heel and ran to her Papa.

By mid-April we'd finished our basic training at the Regimental depot, and within three days, thirty-two recruits including Harry and myself sailed across the Irish Sea to join the 2nd Battalion in Dublin.

For three-and-a-half months we were drilled mercilessly on the parade square, learning additional field-craft and infantry battle wave tactics to the point of exhaustion amongst the hills of County Wicklow.

On the firing ranges we honed our marksmanship skills to devastating effect and woe betide any soldier who didn't achieve a two-inch grouping on the targets at three hundred yards. What seemed to be brutal training with no let-up in the first few weeks became easier over time as our military confidence, fitness and skill at arms grew. We gradually understood that the intense training was preparing us to kill and destroy other men without compunction.

On a most memorable Saturday afternoon in early July, I saw Dorothy for the first time, in a tearoom at the bottom end of Sackville Street.

Fortunately I was in mufti (civilian clothes) which helped a lot when it came to meeting a young lady, as wearing the King's uniform would most likely deter any respectable encounter. The fair city of Dublin and its people were not always convivial towards British soldiers. As I walked in, I noticed her sitting near the bay window engrossed in a book and in an instant I felt ... no, I knew, I definitely knew. She was the most sublime beautiful vision and from that day forth would occupy every recess of my heart and visit me in my dreams. Trying not to stare was difficult, because for the first time in my short life I felt an overwhelming desire to introduce myself but had no idea how. I sat down two tables away from her.

As the waitress took my order, Dorothy lifted her eyes and looked at me.

I could only think the reason for her fleeting interest was my English accent. This brief moment allowed me to smile my best smile at her. She held her composure, not smiling in return, or at least not with her lips. Did my imagination play a trick on me? I was sure her amazing green eyes smiled back at me.

War was declared against Germany on Tuesday 4th August 1914. We immediately mobilised and were shipped to France. Within two weeks we had marched into Belgium as part of the British Expeditionary Force deployed to Mons, thirty-five miles south of Brussels. On Sunday 23rd August we engaged the Germans in deadly combat. Through September, we had to fight several rear-guard actions against the unrelenting advance of the

'Hun' in order to protect our tiny army's desperate withdrawal.

By October we'd moved to the outskirts of a town in West Flanders called Ypres (which the army nicknamed 'Wipers' because it was easier to pronounce).

We battled hard against Fritz for a whole month, giving a good account of ourselves, but inevitably lost a lot of sound blokes, including the hardest man in the battalion. Corporal Farrar, was taken out by a 'potato masher' (a German stick grenade), after he'd bayoneted a three-man machinegun crew single handed. On this glorious sunny morning we tucked into real grub, all the men in our trench lines wolfed down bacon butties and slaked their thirst with mugs of hot sweet tea, fare that wasn't often available to us. Must be a catch…

Later that same glorious sunny morning … Tut-tut-tut-tut-tut-tut-tut-tut! Tut-tut-tut-tut. And again … Tut-tut-tut-tut-tut-tut-tut-tut!

During the second advance towards enemy lines Spandau MG 08's opened up on us, spitting six hundred rounds per minute. Tut-tut-tut-tut-tut-tut-tut-tut!

"TAKE COVAAAR …" screamed Serjeant Johnson, just before he took several jerking thumps to the head and chest, falling like a stone. Ever since we'd landed in France, Harry and I had watched each other's backs and today would be no different. The old 'sweats' used to say "you never hear the one that gets you" but I heard it, in a split second. A hailstorm of hot lead rounds tore into both our bodies.

We crumpled to the ground in a heap of tangled rifles, kit and limbs. I'd been invisibly scythed open, diagonally from shoulder to hip.

My lungs gasped for air; amid agonising, pitiful guttural groans, I desperately tried to formulate words. Harry, having taken hits to his shoulder and thigh, managed to grasp hold of my hand. Fingers grappled with fingers, interweaving ... and then ... peace and calm enveloped my blood-soaked space. My heart slowed down and, for a few moments in the middle of the surrounding din of battle, I heard a voice call out to me: "Walter, I'm here to take you home."

Hovering above me stood a soldier.

His gentle eyes and his smile seemed distantly familiar. He reached out his hand and said, "Walter, it's time to leave this place now."

Coughing gouts of blood and mucus, I moved my lips.

"Got to say goodbye to Harry, I can't leave without saying goodbye."

I turned my head to look at Harry and saw tears tracing lines down and across his dirt-covered face as he silently mouthed words with cracked bloody lips. He was praying ... for me. Tears rolled down my cheeks as I squeezed Harry's hand in a code I knew he would understand, and for a few moments a smile cut across my face as we looked into each other's eyes. Harry couldn't smile; he wailed ... in anguish.

Lying there, my bullet-riddled chest wheezed heavenwards and within a few minutes I bled out next to my best friend. My brother.

I stood up. The soldier placed his hand upon my shoulder, and led me away.

I never experienced the closeness of a woman; marriage, or the joy of having children. I'm sure these wonderful things would have happened, if this madness hadn't descended upon us. Our world was simple, predictable, ordered. Of course flaws and inequalities existed within our world. Harry and I believed we could help it to change, for the better.

But nonetheless it was our world ... our time ... our lives.

Our halcyon days!

PART FOUR
Non-Fiction

What Does It Mean To Be Human
By Joe Larkin

'WHAT DOES IT MEAN TO BE HUMAN?'

BY
JOE LARKIN

(The Drift of Mind)

This essay is my muse on the age-old question: 'What does it mean to be human?' Certainly not to be taken too seriously. This is my essay, my research, my observations and my current understanding, hence the sub-title: 'The Drift of Mind.' I hope you find it interesting.

Heck, what Does It All Mean?
Every human being who comes into this world has no control of 'which side of the bed they are born on,' no more than we have over other factors, such as our given sex in the womb, physical and/or mental defects, colour of our skin, nationality or religion at birth. Is it unfair to have disparity of wealth between rich and poor within society? Some would suggest our lives are predestined, and to a certain degree I go along with that theory. What I do believe is nothing concerning human life can be termed as random. I understand 'things happen' and these 'happenstance' events or accidents are considered by many as random acts of misfortune, when in actual fact (not to be realised at the time) they can in many cases morph towards a positive outcome quickly, or further down the line, sometimes without us ever making the connection.

Lucky or unlucky, rich or poor are adjectives that cause so much confusion and misunderstanding and I argue, these individual words can have debilitating consequences for the people who believe they apply to them, 'life is not fair' and it is as it is.

Furthermore there is no such thing as luck in the real sense. The universe does not contain any luck. Luck is only ever real in the mind-set of individual human beings. 'He was in the wrong place at the wrong time' does not make sense. A person is there because they happen to be there, (pure coincidence), even though we may never understand why. It is not random forces that are in play here but 'cause and effect' which is the true order of our universe.

Inequalities in this world are clearly man made; relative prosperity, education, medical care, sufficient food and water, suitable housing, freedom of speech and expression, freedom of religion and the freedom of peace are not guaranteed (although most right thinking folks would like them to be).

Obtaining wealth through entrepreneurial means, career development and promotional prospects are not randomly handed out to people. The above are obtained by individuals who desire them, and in many cases individuals have to make sacrifices, take risks, paying what they consider to be a high price to achieve their goals.

Humanity's ability to overcome adversity has in my opinion no limits. 'We shall overcome' has been mankind's clarion call since time immemorial and will continue until the end of time!

Having said that I must point out that I'm under no illusion to the fact history has shown us and continues to show that a more powerful (minority) group of the human race (try to) control our lives under the guise of government (democratically elected or not), fiefdoms, powerful lobbying groups representing industrial and commercial corporations and even certain educational systems promoting their own school of thought and ideological agenda.

This is the crux of the argument in relation to inequality. I have heard it said many times, the world we live in can adequately feed all of its 7 billion plus inhabitant's year in year out with plenty of food in reserve if only a more humane egalitarian attitude existed within the most powerful governments around the world. This is patently not the case. The above hypothesis is not some naive unproven liberalistic ideal. On the contrary enlightened people and worthy organisations have advocated this humane way of thinking for many years. To name just a few:

Pope Leo XIII's encyclical letter of 1891 'Rerum Novarum' (The 7 Principals of Catholic Social Teaching); 1. Life & Dignity of the Human Person, 2. Call to Family, Community & Participation, 3.Rights & Responsibilities, 4. Options for the Poor & Vulnerable, 5. The Dignity of Work & the Rights of Workers, 6. Solidarity, 7. Care for God's Creation.

The United Nations *Declaration of Human Rights* adopted by the UN General Assembly on 10th December 1948 *'guarantees the rights of every individual everywhere.'*

The International Labour Organisation World Employment Programme submitted the basic document *'Employment Growth and Basic Needs a One World Problem'* to the 1976 ILO World Employment Conference.

Inequalities and disparity exist in our world of rich and poor; however I do believe humanity has the ability to achieve justice and equality for all, although it seems for the foreseeable future to be a 'work in progress.' Oft quoted; *'All that is necessary for the triumph of evil is that good men do nothing'* Edmund Burke (1729-1797) and a quotation I particularly favour *'The evil of the world is made possible by nothing but the sanction you give it.* Ayn Rand (1905-1980). I reiterate, there is no 'right or wrong side' of the bed to be born on and therefore the realisation that there are no absolute guarantees in life (other than death itself) allows for clarity, and helps us strive to be brave, therefore making us more human, and the answer to what does it all mean?
'Life is either a daring adventure or nothing. Security does not exist in nature, nor do the children as a whole, experience it. Avoiding danger is no safer in the long run than exposure.' Helen Keller *(1880-1968).*

In the following (and with an element of creative licence) I have attempted to give another interpretation of the continual quest 'what does it means to be human?' by studying a photograph called: *'How can I worry about the damned dishes when there are children dying in Vietnam?' by Bill Owens from his book Suburbia (1972)*

The photograph shows a young mother holding her infant son in a kitchen.

It has been estimated by the Vietnamese Government that a total of 84,000 children died during the Vietnam War with the United States of America.

They died from massive US Air Force ariel bombardments, totalling 7,800,000 tons of ordinance dropped on their homes, villages and towns.

Combining the Air Force tonnage with the Army and Navy's munitions, the sum total is 15,500,000 tons spent. Along with an *'Agent Orange Dioxin Herbicidal Warfare'* strategy, a legacy has resulted in a continuing stream of Vietnamese children born to this very day with birth defects (including 2nd & 3rd generations), estimated at a staggering figure of 500,000, since the end of the war in 1975. And on top of these grotesque numbers sits approximately 800,000 children made orphans throughout the war because of man's inhumanity towards his fellow man.

Hence the soul searching by the young mother in Owens black and white suburban photograph of 1972, somewhere in 'Normalsville, US of A.'

My imagination wants me to give this intense early 1970's all American urbanite mother a name. So I'm going to call her Lori Jo Jimbrowski and her 'fat lil cutesy boy' will be called Jimmy Brett Jimbrowski. By identifying the two protagonists I wish to explore the burning question a little further, hopefully exposing paradigms of human thoughtlessness to actually be a form of acquiescing. The notion is 'I think therefore I am' ... I am human, however the opposite side of the same coin reads: 'I think less, therefore I am' Am I still human?

Lori is a mother who is going through a mildly maudlin metamorphosis in relation to how she sees the world she is living in, and the world she's brought JB into. So much so, on the day this photograph was taken of her and JB in the kitchen her worries and concerns about the world in general, and in particular the children in Vietnam, gives her a plausible humane excuse in avoiding her domestic chores.

Only a few minutes before, she anxiously watched Walter Cronkite ('The most trusted man in America') broadcast journalist and anchorman for CBS TV, soberly broadcast the latest news on the success of the US Air Force's *'Operation Linebacker 2's'* Ariel bombing campaign, against strategic targets in North Vietnam.

They dropped 20,000+ tons of bombs from B52 Stratofortress heavy bomber planes which resulted in the deaths of 1,624 civilians, many of them children. Interestingly enough later on in the US Pentagon's military debriefing it couldn't be established how many North Vietnamese military personnel were killed. Lori got up from the sofa, with a not so little JB in her arms, muttering to herself 'How can I worry about the damned dishes when there are children dying in Vietnam?' Lori slept fitfully that night.

Now we fast forward to March 2003 and sadly Lori is all alone, sitting in her lounge watching the 'Shock and Awe' of America's latest 'good cop, bad cop' routine unfolding over the skies of Iraq on her favourite news channel CBS.

She anxiously listens to Dan Rather the incumbent news anchorman reporting that the US 3rd Marine Aircraft Wing USMC (of which her 'cutesy beefcake all American boy' Major Jimmy Brett Jimbrowski is an F/A-18 Hornet jet fighter pilot) have just bombed the 'heck outta' Baghdad City dropping 23,000 GPB's (General Purpose Bombs) and 22,000 PGM's (Precision Guided Munitions) over the course of a few days.

Lori is so proud of her boy and prays to God that he comes home safe and sound and in the meantime she hopes he will phone her soon, as she does worry so. Jimmy on the other hand is in a jubilant mood, now back from his mission and chilling out with his 'bro pilots' in his unit accommodation on the sprawling *'Al Jaber'* Air Base in the Kuwaiti desert. *'Kill Anything That Moves,'* the 3rds unofficial motto is painted above the entrance to the unit TV room where Jimmy and his bro's are watching

Dan Rather present the same news item his mother is watching in real time, stateside.

The guys all laugh loudly and josh each other over the news footage giving quick glimpses of unit characters stepping down from their Hornets posing *'Top Gun'* style for the CBS cameras.

'OORAH.' The news item finishes and Lori rises from her La-Z-Boy recliner and heads for the kitchen to tidy up. She loads up her dish washer and sets it to wash, and for a moment she muses (a wry smile on her face) over the fact she doesn't have to worry about the damned dishes anymore!

PART FIVE
Poetry

To Those I Have
By Ange Dunn

Ephemeral Verse
By Chris Robinson

Memories
By Irene Styles

Into The Trees
By Irene Styles

Breaking Up
By Kevin Horsley

A Song for the Suburbs
By T.H.

Last Words
By T.H.

Photo Album
By T.H.

Seabird
By T.H.

TO THOSE I HAVE LOVED AND LOST

BY
ANGE DUNN

Inspired by the Gloria Gaynor song I Will Survive.

At first I was afraid I was petrified,
I kept thinking 'Who is next? How does it
decide?'
I spent so many nights thinking that life was so
wrong,
but I grew strong when I heard that old special
song.

But one day the song I went to listen
and then I realised what it was that was
missing,
and with that realisation I began to cry,
and I couldn't pull myself together. Why did you
have to die?

The reasons, well they were all in my brain,
but to speak them out aloud would cause so
much more pain.
Everyday it gets worse, more than I can bare,
knowing that there's stuff in my life that you will
never get to share.

I wish you didn't have to die like this,
that I instead of you had received deaths kiss.
I wish the Angels took me instead of you,
your life was ahead of you all shiny and new.

It's not fair, it's not right,
but I know that you would have put up the fight.
So I hope that you're at peace
and that you finally got your sweet release.

But the freak show of life still goes on
and I'm going to cause a riot before my time
has gone.
So, to you all up in that castle in the sky,
I'm saying night-night, sweet dreams and
Goodbye.

Its time to be moving on,
to start my life with a brand new song.
I won't forget,
but there is no time to regret

And each and every one of you I truly will miss,
but I can't afford to reminisce.
I won't stop trying,
I will try to keep on smiling,
but 'till a cure for that cancer is found I won't
easily rest,
because it took away some of my heroes; the
greatest and the best!

EPHEMERAL VERSE

BY
CHRIS ROBINSON

You'll have heard me before;
I'm a bit of a bore,
Though you've probably come across worse.
More typic than tragic,
Not mystic, not magic.
My name is ephemeral verse.

It's hard to outline,
Or describe or define
What tradition precisely I fit.
More exactly, I fill
Every space on the bill,
Where no other traditions are it.

When all depth is all doubt,
And all insight is out,
And incisiveness cuts like a knife;
When your mind, casting round
Casts out the profound,
And you've heard quite enough about life.

I will furnish an ode,
Not a clue, not a code
Hidden meaning or reading initial,
Expressly designed
To leave nothing behind.
But a sense of the sense superficial

When my surface is skimmed,
And the reading lamp dimmed,
And depressing reflections appear
The thought does persist
That I need not exist,
Until I remember I'm here.

THE HALIBURTON GIRLS

Rachael was born in Glamorgan,
Heather was born in West Eight,
Their nurse pushed a pram in Seringapatam
Where the family encamped at the call of the
state;

Rachael I met through a mutual friend
At a party where jobs were discussed;
A modern art gallery paid her a salary
Based (so she claimed) on the size of her bust;

We didn't get on like a house that's on fire,
But our eyes were quite well double-glazed
When they ran out of wine and she asked me
to dine
With her sister and her in a couple of days.

If Rachael was terribly, terribly,
Heather was terribly, too.
She towed an old beau who approached her as
though
He'd seduced her at tennis when tennis was
new.

There was very much talk of inflation
And of whether abortion was good;

There was talk of a sister who lived in a blister
As part of a project to prove that one could;

The lady beside me at dinner
Did research into juvenile crime
And it started to strike me she possibly liked
me.
(She said I was wonderful twenty-four times).

But, in twenty-four hours, in Paris,
Where I'd gone for a week and a day,
While selling computers to business school
tutors,
I met the two girls in the Rue de la Paix.

Rachael looked cute in a silk boiler suit,
And Heather in leather was cool;
The tennis-club fellow stood blazered in yellow
Beside a mad Earl played by Peter O'Toole:

We said to each other "How are you?"
The gentlemen jiggled their shades,
And they asked me to join them down in the
Dordogne,
But I stuck to my synthetic fibre and stayed.

I computed the world and encountered a girl
In a boat on the Caspian Sea;
It was clear from her cleaner, demurer
demeanour,
No jangly, bangly, hippy was she.

My curious bent was un-bended,
My impressionable nature, impressed.
The Turk at the tiller there called her Camilla,

Her surname I somehow quite suddenly
guessed.

The little boat landed in shallows well-sanded,
We soon left the shore far behind.
And by double decision there reached a
position where
Blisters were very remote from our mind.

We married, and after a journey of laughter,
Set up on the banks of the Rhone.
I live with Camilla in part of a villa
We rent from the don in the part that we don't.

We've wonderful cheese in the cellar,
And excellent wine on the rack,
And when Rachael and Heather pay visits
together
They're lively as ever (until they go back).

We survey the fine country around us
Through our railings, wrought-iron, antique;
Which we know will preserve us from any
observers
Apart from the one that's delivered each week.

Now I find that my mind is a mirror,
With reflections I'd rather forget.
I've reflected red lights in pursuit of delights,
And I've had an affair with a drum majorette.

I've courted a kibbutz commander,
And pointed her back to the land.
I've grappled with geishas in manner so
gracious

I couldn't imagine I'd an edge to my hand.

I've nosed with an Eskimo lady,
And I've necked with a woman from Dar;
And after a nightful, I found them delightful,
As far as they went (and they went pretty far).

But, speaking as one who has seen a few
things and as someone who's easily bored,
This planet is brimming with wonderful women,
But give me a county girl, living abroad.

THE OLD CONSUMABLES.

A little fridge lay dying,
It quivered on its side.
No food was left upon its shelves,
Its door was open wide.

It looked around the scrapyard
And saw a fearful sight.
Above the flood of wreckage, stood
The crusher, clean and bright.

Its levers all were gleaming;
Its piston, trim and square.
No patch of rust of speck of dust
Its function did impair.

To feed its hungry orifice
A broad conveyor surged.
The steel and tin were fed within
And little cubes emerged.

This prospect for the little fridge

Filled all its tubes with gall,
"There was no need to dump me here,
A faulty valve was all

That had to be replaced, and I'd
Have gone on working well.
'Twas pure and simple fridgicide
To dump me in this hell!

Their food I kept in sterile store
And white wine, fit for Bacchus.
And then, when I broke down, they swore,
And sent me to the knackers!"

The fridge's angry warning light
With fury flickered on;
Reflect the sunset thought it might,
Its inner power was gone.

Its shiny white enamel skin
Was clammy with the dew.
Far colder now outside than in,
Its melancholy grew.

Just then a larger fridge slid by,
And, stopping with a bump,
With interest great, perused the plate
Upon the small one's pump.

A moment passed, then with a blast
Of cold air in the night,
The large antique began to speak
In accents clear and bright.

"I see your reference number

Is very close to mine.
You must have been assembled on
The next production line.

I'm glad you're here; my hopes had sunk
My wits were at an end;
With all this cheap imported junk
It's good to find a friend."

So, side by side, both far and wide
Their conversation ranged
As memories gay of younger days
Were happily exchanged.

"Remember Fred the foreman?"
The large appliance said,
"That day he went to free a vent
And banged his silly head?"

"Remember Sid the charge-hand?"
The smaller one replied.
"When only nine turned up on time,
He very nearly died!"

After a moment's silence, when
The chatter had subsided,
The small to the capacious fridge
Its deep despair confided.

The big fridge puffed its cooling pipe
And pursed its rubber seal:
"Though some," it said, "would count us dead,
I'll tell you what I feel."

I've read instruction manuals,

And magazines, and feel
The Great White Kitchen in The Sky
Is just a fond ideal."

"You see them in advertisements
All shining spick and span;
I don't believe them, and don't see
How anybody can."

"But steel can't turn to nothing; that
Makes nonsense of creation;
The truth to me is plain to see,
It is - reincarnation."

"The crusher can't destroy a thing,
But merely bends, and fractures;
From there we go to join the flow
Of newer manufactures."

"In your next life you could make up
A fridge, as you now are;
An aeroplane, a boat or train,
A scooter or a car."

"Myself, I'm sick to death of storing
Meat and veg and cola;
When the crusher hits, I hope my bits
Will form a Merc or Roller."

"Back there I met a doctor's fridge
Who's also come to this.
While I'm pissed off with keeping cheese;
He's cheesed off keeping piss."

"I'll try to cope, and live in hope,"

The little fridge then stated.
"I'm feeling tired, but more inspired,
In fact, I'm quite elated."

The daylight came, and in its train
The morning shift drew nigh.
With a flash of pain the magnet crane
Lifted them both on high.

The big fridge took the little fridge
And held its handle tight.
"No time to grieve!" it said, "believe
In what I said last night!"

Then, placed on the conveyor,
And hustled fast along,
Not in despair, but debonair,
They sang a cheerful song.

The other scrap joined in with them;
The words they sang were these:
(In German, Dutch, Italian, Spanish,
Hindi and Chinese)

OLD CONSUMER DURABLES!
MARCHING NOW TO REST!
WARRANTY ENDURABLES!
PASSED THE FINAL TEST!

AGE MAY DIM OUR BEAUTY
WASHED BY TIME AND TIDE
FIT FOR HEAVY DUTY
ON WE'LL ALWAYS RIDE!

TILL THE TRUMPET CALLS
AND GUARANTEE EXPIRES -
THEN, SCRAP METAL, WE SHALL FALL

TO FEED BLAST FURNACE FIRES!

AND RISE AGAIN! RISE AGAIN!
UNTOUCHED BY ALL DECAY!
CONSUMER DURABLES NEVER DIE -
THEY ONLY MELT AWAY....

WHAT HAPPENED TO DAPHNE CARRUTHERS?

What happened to Daphne Carruthers
When she had come into High Hall?
And Bunty Maltravers, the others?
Whatever became of them all?

That wild-eyed young orphan called Harry,
We found out was Albemarle's son.
Did he ever make good, or marry?
His story had barely begun.

The linguist, whose missing pyjamas
Were such a significant clue,
Who went to Tibet to meet lamas;
I don't know what happened. Do you?

The Vicar, Lance couldn't quite throttle
Because the churchwarden arrived.
Did he ever give up the bottle,
And preach about how he'd survived?

That pair, one in shirts, one in blouses;
Whose claim to be sisters was thin:
(The cut of the mannish one's trousers;
 The big Brylcreem jar in the bin...)

Were they ever happily outed

As kinder conventions arose,
And flaunted where once they had flouted,
In Notting Hill ... Newark ... Who knows?

In matters of prognostication
Where nothing is clear, cut and dry;
In place of precise information,
The laws of statistics apply.

So, what happened to Daphne Carruthers,
And her other companions, perforce?
Why, in one of their tales or one other's
The whole lot were murdered, of course.

A SONG,
IN PRAISE OF AUTOMATIC DOORS

I want to sing a song in praise of automatic
doors
In libraries and vestibules and nice department
stores
Which, as your feet approach, informed by mat
or magic eye
Will gently glide apart for you while uttering a
sigh.

A subtle swish, out-rustling the leaves in
summer trees;
A shuffling sound like paper in sublime
bureaucracies.
Compliant purrs no cat or master diplomat
could match
Accompany each movement, back and forth, in
due dispatch.

Bag-laden shoppers come and go, bag-laden still, but stately.
Book-bearing readers bear their books this way and that, sedately.
No pushing with their toes for them, no knob to fumble for,
Their simple motion motivates the automatic door.

How wonderful would be this world, and human life be bliss,
If all transitions otherwise were smooth as silk as this!
No card to swipe, no form to fill; no declaration made;
No pin tapped out; no status sought, no fee that must be paid.

No test to pass, no stage to reach, legalities to heed;
No notifying change of state, no manual to read,
No statement of necessity, no claimed effect or cause.
I therefore shout my song in praise of automatic doors.

THINGS I WILL LEAVE WHEN I DIE.

My banjo-ukelele, seldom played;
My 'Reader's Guide' to something, seldom read,
My book of things to make, but seldom made,
Some words I often thought, but seldom said.

The stone I picked beside a waterfall,
The twig that looked like someone Lowry saw,
The leaf that fell upon my head, and all
The little objects jumbled in the drawer.

The frames I made for some old prints of mine,
Quite good, but all too clearly done at home;
Some drawings with some slight control of line,
A half unfinished tin of shaving foam.

These things I'll leave behind me when I die'
Once bought or brought, again to bring and
buy.
SENSATIONS

The smell of bonfires ageing,
The sound of twittering skies,
The sight of plums, presaging
The taste of new plum pies.

The touch of winter, gnarling
The tree of old despair;
And my sixth sense, my darling,
Is neither here nor there.

For here is not Mauritius,
And there, not Boreham Wood;
And you are there, my precious,
And I am here, for good.

HARTLEPOOL SONNET

Pick up a shell and put it to your ear
And hear the murmur of the morning tide.
Then catch the woeful, whining, whistling fear

Of shells from German battle-cruisers fired.

Note the old wreck protruding from the silt;
That's more than two vast steelworks came to
be.
There's one atomic power station built
Beside a beach where coal's washed up for
free.

A hanging monkey dangled in the air
While Britain fought Napoleonic Wars.
The monkey then became a monkey mayor
Elected thrice to general applause.

With all these wonders plain for all to see,
What town could ever need mythology?

SOME SHELLS TOGETHER WITH
ELASTIC BAND

Some shells together with elastic band;
The three of them in conference on the sea;
The rubber represents the shifting sand;
The shells debate the tide's complicity.

In huddled caucus, open mouth to mouth
Their bony outer casings crinkled, curled,
A globe make up, with east, west, north and
south;
A solid surface turned against the world.
No outer sign that they were once alive;
No sense of space in matter tightly packed;
A $CaCo3$ times M.I.5;
A carbonate official secrets act.

But put them back upon the silver shore,
Where rubber, shell are smashed by sun and
sea,
Their precious secrets then will be no more;
Their subject, sand, their information, free.

SEATON BEACH.

I'm going back to Seaton Beach,
I'm tired of being out of reach,
Beyond the tides of life, I'll find
The ocean left behind.

I'll sit upon the sand at night,
And pull the sea to pale moonlight,
And every drop will then contain
The spectrum of my brain.

I'll hear the hard wind catch the dunes
And strum the grass to softer tunes

Sometimes I'll wonder through the town
As just another proper noun
Lost in the queue and on the dole
The jetsam of my soul.

But then I'll take the sea as well,
Become another kind of shell,
Reclassified and redefined
The flotsam of my mind.

Beach comb a future for my past
And then I'll know I'm home at last.

So I'm returning to the womb

I'm filling out and finding room
To bathe awhile and breathe the air,
And Sheila will be there.

LYNN STREET BLUES.

The cakeshop on the corner
Isn't baking any longer,
It's a superseded corner store.
Nobody lives there any more.
Buying the buns
And the sweet Sally Lunns,
The customers came and spent,
Went, and came back again,
In the sun and the rain.
Whatever the weather,
Coming for more
And more and more and no more.

The woman at the corner
Isn't waiting any longer,
She's a superseded corner whore.
Nobody loves her any more.
Strutting her stuff
With the smooth and the rough,
The clientele came and spent,
Went,
And came back again
In the sun and the rain,
Whatever the weather,
Coming for more.
And more and more and no more.

The neon signs are swaying
And the Empire is decaying,

It's a superseded music hall
Nobody laughs there any more.

Full to the hilt,
From the gods to the gilt,
The audience came and spent,
Went,
And came back again,
In the sun and the rain,
Whatever the weather
Roaring for more,
And more and more and no more.

BOUNCING BACK

We'd had one minor hit in 'sixty-nine;
The group broke up (we called them groups
back then);
They'd called us Geordies; we'd said "Tees,
not Tyne!"
They'd not known where, and now they don't
know when.
I'm not surprised, though, when I count the
years
(While trying not to count the cost), because
To them, when my age was the same as theirs,
I must be older than George Formby was.
And now I'm stuck on the Transporter Bridge
To jump and show a bungee break my fall,
My mind a mass of fear, my feet a fridge,
My cause, a charity I can't recall.
My only friend a television chap
Who got my name right on the sixth re-take;
While eighty new acquaintances may clap
Routinely, if the bungee doesn't break.

They did applaud the last one quite a lot,
And went on while they disengaged the rope,
But then he's just been murdered in the plot
Of some crime drama, serial or soap.
The jumper after me caused quite a buzz,
When they announced his name an hour ago;
He sounds just like the shipping forecast does;
I think he runs an all-night phone-in show.
It looks as though his fan club's on its way;
A crowd of aimless punters looking dim;
They've doubtless just awoken for the day.
They look at me as if they think I'm him.

They say that, just before you're really dead
Your whole life flashes past, and then you're
gone;
And, though I know I'm set to bounce instead,
There's quite a lot of flashing going on.

The telly chap has just called out my name;
I'm quite surprised he got it right, not wrong;
Almost as though he's playing some strange
game,
Almost as though he knew it all along.
Since they've announced me, now's the time I
guess,
It's to the edge, and don't look down, and jump
And ah! And oh! And no! And oh!
And yes! And bend! And bounce! And up! And
down! And bump!
And bump?
Not bump, another word instead;
Not bump? Not bump, but hit, our minor hit.
I'm in the air. They're cheering. I'm not dead.
And thousands down below are singing it.

IT ISN'T QUITE DONE IN THE MIDDLE

I was sitting one day in the kitchen,
My mother was doing her chores;
A traditional wife, giving lessons of life
With her homely old wisdom and time-
honoured lore.
With a well-practised push of a button
The microwave door would obey.
She would touch and would feel her
convenience meal,
And these wise words my mother would say:

"It isn't quite done in the middle.
In the middle it isn't quite done.
The breadcrumbs are golden, the cheddar is
molten,
But inside it's frozen as hard as the tundra.
The top and the bottom are glowing
And the corners all smoke like a gun.
But it isn't quite done in the middle, my son.
In the middle it isn't quite done."

"It isn't quite done in the middle"
I recalled when my mother had gone.
When I looked at the cricket, and saw at the
wicket
A streaker exposing his silly mid-on.
For to prance around more or less naked
On the edge of the field, may be fun.
But it isn't quite done in the middle, my son,
In the middle it isn't quite done.

"It isn't quite done in the middle"

When political speeches are heard;
Hear the shouts and the screams that expound
both extremes
While all moderate men of goodwill mince their
words.
For a top cannot whistle nor wobble
When a sensible spin's to be spun;
No, it isn't quite done in the middle, my son
In the middle it isn't quite done.

"It isn't quite done in the middle"
Why, it's true of the world as a whole;
Where a Peer of the Realm may get high as an
elm,
And the poor lower orders may drink all their
dole,
The bourgeois has no such protection
He must hide in his home to have fun.
For it isn't quite done in the middle, my son
In the middle it isn't quite done.

THE PRO's

May we interpose
If we may?
We're the PRO's
That's to say
We'll help you hold a pose
In a world where anything goes.
We're the PRO's.

Imagine the facts as an ice-cube.
Imagine the fiction as gin.
The facts slide about
In a bucket of doubt

Till we take them with tongs and deposit them
in.
Before half a lunch conversation,
Before half a concept takes wings.
The ice and the booze
And the falses and trues
Will be mingled before the cash register rings.

We take tame reporters out
Eating then;
If they claim they've caught us out
Cheating, then
We would never shout,
Explete, delete or tread toes.
We're the PRO's.

In this world where an apple's an orange,
In this game where a ball is a bat,
Where all reason is rhyme at this moment in
time,
And a failure is anything other than that,
You'll appreciate why we are needed,
To convey, in a cart that's a horse,
The approximate truth
With a marital ruth
To a public that privately wants a divorce.
And though we may defy grammarians
And treat the language like barbarians,
We'll never tell a lie -
Though, sometimes, we're at variance...
Absolutely, basically yours,
We're the PRO's.

LIMERICKS.

An intelligent lemming named Crichton
Whom the rush to the sea used to frighten,
Found his progress was slowed
If he travelled by road
Like the humans, from London to Brighton.

~~~~~~

An opera singer named Betty
Once fell in a vat of spaghetti,
And then, while they freed her
Sang 'Faust' and 'Aida'
(With slightly adapted libretti).

~~~~~~

A grumpy old lion of Judah
Grew tired of his trainer, and sued her;
But she wasn't impressed
By dismissal thus stressed;
So he chewed her and chewed her and
chewed her.

~~~~~~

A girl with a girdle from Dorset
Died suddenly trying to force it.
Her doctor, when sought
By the coroner's court,
Said: "Of course it's a cause, it's a corset."

~~~~~~

The binary folk of Halesowen
Had no number three, four and so on:
They all lived in two queues
For their two public loos
Which is not very many to go on.

~~~~~~

At the Ritz, an old bishop called "Waiter!
I've got an enormous potato!"

The reply: "All my life
I've had one called my wife,
And I wouldn't complain if you ate her."

~~~~~~

A bookworm, to answer a bet,
Persevered all the way through Debrett
And at page eighty-three,
Discovered that he
Was in line for an Earl's coronet.

~~~~~~

When the other worms watching him saw
The stiff upper lip he now wore
And enquired of their Lord
How he found his reward,
He said "Find it a bit of a bore".

~~~~~~

A very well-off undertaker
Had a mistress, and couldn't forsake her
On expense-account cruises
He'd enter her dues as
"A coffin en route from Jamaica".

Once there, when the ship had conveyed him,
An ancient clairvoyant waylaid him
And said "You should know
With arrival you'll go,
And in two ways, not one," which dismayed
him.

That night, still awake, he reflected
On what the clairvoyant projected:
How, arriving, he'd go,
He found no way to know,
And returned home to Dorking dejected.

Next day the Inspector of Taxes
(Who hardly, if ever, relaxes)
Decided to pounce
On his flimsy accounts
And proceeded to grind a few axes.

"I'll tell you in brief what my task is,"
He said, his face much as a mask is,
"My concern is provoked
By these cargoes of croaked;
The reason for which, may I ask, is?"

The poor man broke into a fever
Called in the official receiver
Fled Surrey mock-tudor
For sunny Bermuda
And took an account in Geneva.

Without time to unpack his pyjamas
He was dealt the most poignant of dramas.
On arrival, he died,
And upon the next tide,
Was returned to a rival embalmers.

GIVE ME THE KEY TO THE DOOR OF YOUR HEART

Give me the key to the door of your heart;
Show me the door of the key;
Clink in the lock of the door of the start;
End in the castle with me.
Joy is the jewel that's set in the heart;
Love is the lustre that gleams;
Dancing on doors which once kept us apart,
Hung on the hinge of our dreams.

MEMORIES

BY
IRENE STYLES

Pictures of my younger self,
Carefree days, childhood memories,
Cherished and tucked safely away
To draw upon when life seems grey.

We climbed the snow-covered hill
Dragging the wooden sled behind us.
Flakes of sparkling white fell, melting
On icy nose tips and poked-out tongues.
Clouds of steamy breath, puffed white
From chapped lips as we ploughed ever on,
Feet sunk deep into the snowy carpet.
We were exultant, looking forward to the ride
back down,

Giggling and squealing we picked up speed,
Bumping over ruts and snow-cased hillocks of
grass,
Wind blasted, hair thrown back behind us,
Tears streaming, frozen on rose-tinged
cheeks.
All caution abandoned; the sled sped as we
fled homeward.
Then under the darkening sky, we traversed
the hill one last time,

Making the most of that happy, snow-filled day.
Knowing Spring was just around the corner -

The white blanket melting into green, as
Rain, sweet and fresh, dripped
Onto buds struggling through the earth
And rippled pools,
To splash our shiny black wellingtons.

INTO THE TREES

BY
IRENE STYLES

I can't go to any other place
I'm island bound
An island of trees
Even in the distant sea
Logs abound from fallen trees, bobbing,
sinking, resurfacing,
Glistening like hump back whales come close
to shore,
to entertain ferry passengers, rushing to the
rusted rails, fingers pointing,
excited voices directing, then disappointed
tones ring out -
'It's only a log!'
From pebbled shore to black, misted mountain
tops pines tall, lush, green,
blanket every inch of land.
Bald headed eagles, circle and dive, carry
twitching prey off into the trees,
Grizzly bears with cubs, shuffle and dartanda
giant antlered moose lumbers, on the hunt for
food into the trees.
Hikers find winding trails, branches and fallen
leaves crackling underfoot, guiding them
through trees of lush wood in search of wildlife
and panoramic views.
In cultivated gaps houses spring up, always
overshadowed by trees, sun-dappled light
brightens timbered rooms.

Gardens filled with plants that deer will not
feast upon,
Finding nothing they return to the trees, and
the rutting stags call.
At night there are no lights and trees block the
moon and stars,
The dark is deep and thick, as we walk with
hand held torches to lead the way,
going home and always, always, into, the trees.

BREAKING UP

BY
KEVIN HORSLEY

I remember that first time you approached
through the dry ice and laughter, just a friends
friend back then.

And we talked of ... music, cinema, film
literature, our likes and dislikes.

We met as friends for weeks, the thought of
more on my mind; I asked ... you declined.

But I gave you my number, which you took
and called me some weeks later and arranged
a date, late January.

A film I recall and then a slow walk to the taxi
rank, our minds alight setting the world to
rights.

A lingering kiss stayed on my lips and in my
dreams; as we parted something grand had
started.

There were many more dates which I recall,
with perfection, heedless of circumspection.

For I had found love and it had found me. I felt
lighter, unencumbered.

I'm not sure when the great times ended.
I thought we were exempt from familiarity
breeds contempt.

But I was wrong; we'd took each other for
granted and it lead to ... this ... this ...

This limbo where emotions are on hold; I
thought I could rely on your shoulder to cry on.

Because this hurts: this non-existence, it hurts
that we don't talk; it hurts that we'd rather walk
... away.

You on day shift, me on nights, avoiding the
light that perchance I might run into you with
someone new, who is sharing you in ways I
used to do.

And in what we were, what we had; our plans,
dreams, desires; cold nights of warm fires.

And the talking, the talking I thought had no
end; the pure delight of my best friend.

All gone and all that remains are photos and
memories.

A SONG FOR THE SUBURBS

BY
T.H.

'On either side the river lie
Long fields of barley and of rye
That clothe the wolds'
Until
The property speculators came along
And bought the landscape for a song.
They claimed it was a brown land site
Here's ten thousand, that'll fix it, right?
Thus money has the season's power
To change Nature's colours within an hour.
And when they had the magic papers,
Reapers gave way to landscape rapers.
Where nature's glories once did amaze
Investors hath purlieus and rights to graze.
Soon office block call centres rise
Footed in graft, touching the skies.
The purling stream where fishers once
      the lazing bream would lure
Man's ingenuity
      has transformed to a highly effective
              sewer.
And the riverside where lovers strolled
      And perchance would softly kiss
Now flows with turds, used condoms,
      On a gushing stream of piss
Palladio, Lloyd Wright spin in the grave
While modern critics gasp and rave.
It's so bijou, so ... des res

Where it will end is anyone's guess
But as for now. Lord! What a mess!!

LAST WORDS

BY
T.H.

Take down the family bible
Leather binding creaks open
There, first page
Read the record.

'Margaret, daughter of the above
born 23rd June, 1867'
My name, my mother's hand.
Royal Blue Waterman's ink
Fading to grey
At the edges
And then a gap.
'Meg' Mam called me,
(Too many Maggies in Old Town.)

I did not know
How men's hatred
Could fill the sky with fire
And let fall
Sharp
Iron
Rain.

I bled by that beach
Died sprawled across
Those iron rail tracks
Died for a bucket
Of shining black pebbles
To spit and crack
In the grate.

Tonight that hearth
        lies cold
Tonight another hand
Will fill that space
Close my span
Write 'Killed 16 December, 1914'
      In ink as fresh
           and black
              as grief

PHOTO ALBUM

BY
T.H.

In memory of the Rev. James Pattison

The Quakers in
        their Serious garb
    are gone
To happy holy days
    in peaceful graves.

The hitch-skirted girls
    no more
    with bleeding fingers
    hunt the bait.

The fisher-wife
    wrinkled
        beyond her seventy summers
        drops the rake
        from her salt-chapped hand.

His glass plates cracked
    and faded
Collodion seeped
        into sand.
    to a higher calling
    The curate has
        moved on.

Still the wind spears
    across the waves
  Rattles the tough
        marram stalks
    Banked along the Snooks

Just another
    Seaton summer day.

SEABIRD

BY
T.H.

She wakes to a deadened sun
A green curtain across the sky
A viscous drizzle
like dew
but deadly.

She stretches her neck
Croaks her "I'm coming" cry
Fumes choke her voice
Her muscles force her wings
to beat against this captivity.

Who by night snared her unawares'?
Caught in this trap
That is neither metal
nor wire nor wooden cage
but slick like a burning coat
gleaming in fluid rainbows
as it slicks down her feathers
and anchors her to the
gray slow-pulsing sea.

Instinct drives her
Yellow beak burrows
Into matted feathers.
But already oil has seeped
        through the plumage
        to her skin

Already oil is working as acid
      oil is corroding her gullet
      oil is sucking the red
          strength of her blood.

Useless the heft of the wing beat.
Useless the desperate
Plashing of her feet in slime.
She cannot tear her body free.

Sinking, she gives her body
      To the thick tide
Trusting to tomorrow
And the balm of the all healing sea.

Tomorrow carries
A greyed lump
Onto the black sand

Eyes open filmed in yellow.
Neck a tarred coil.
It lifts and droops
Lifts and drops.
Caught on a sluggish pulse
A decayed fish
Tempts the clenched beak.

PART SIX
Romance

Losing Each Other as Friends
By Ange Dunn

Love Stories
By Denise Sparrowhawk

LOSING EACH OTHER AS FRIENDS

BY
ANGE DUNN

All was quiet in the professional flat share. Clara was out on yet another date. Jonathan and Sam were on the late shift and Becky was working late again. That depressed Stefano a little bit but he was growing used to it. It was one of the perils of working within the NHS; patients had to come first.

It was something they all understood and accepted when they joined the service. However, Bec (as he secretly called her) had called to say she was finally on her way home. At least she was not too late this time and she would be home by eight o'clock. An attempt at a nice evening could still be salvaged.

Stefano, knowing Becky as he did, suspected she would have consumed very little of nutritious value since her breakfast of coffee and juice grabbed at 5am that morning. He was going to try and make up for her lack of calorie intake.

Maybe that was the Italian in him, or maybe he was just trying to impress her. If he was asked, he would not be able to give a clear answer.

He would probably try to argue that he just liked to cook the food that his mum had taught him, as a way to alleviate the home sickness he now felt. Either way, food had been made and, even by his own admission, the vivid colours of his homemade meal looked good.

Stefano had just finished serving up when he heard Becky come in. Or rather he heard the flimsy PVC door opening and the sound of her battered, red backpack come flying through it, landing with a crash along with her angry muttering.

"Stefano, you here?" she yelled.

"Yes, in the kitchen; dinner is almost ready." He replied as she came in.

"You hungry?"

"A bit." She replied, as the smell of garlic hit her nostrils making her stomach audibly growl. She was actually starving but not about to admit that to Stefano, no matter how good she thought the food smelt.

"Sit down, sit." he encouraged before turning to her. "Oh, somebody looks unhappy. Not so good day at work?"

"We lost a kid to an RTA. Driver came in with a bad attitude, a bottle of whisky and a broken leg."

Stefano brought the plates over with a sympathetic sigh. "The kids are always the worst ones to deal with."

"Yeah." Becky replied sounding glum.

"Want to talk about it?" Stefano asked sympathetically. He could relate having had a similar experience on his own Accident and Emergency rotation.

"No, I just want to eat, get drunk and just try and forget that horror show." She told him. Stefano's response was to silently get the bottle of wine they kept in stock for such occasions.

The rest of the meal was eaten in relative silence. Stefano trying to make conversation with her, but something was definitely on her mind. It was not only the fact she was having a terrible time at work that was to blame. The realization she never saw, really saw, Stefano anymore, or so it seemed, was also bothering her.

She was having feelings towards Stefano that were more than just wanting to be good friends with him. She was uncertain if he felt the same way, since she was sure she wasn't 'his type'. It was so frustrating for her, especially as he had admitted he loved her, though under heavy anaesthetic thanks to a troublesome tooth removal at the time. Then there was her own embarrassing confession blurted out in her sleep he had teased her about. If only one of them was brave enough to actually admit their feelings for each other, whilst conscious, then maybe things would have been much less confusing.

"Penny for them?" Stefano asked as he watched Becky become lost in thought.

"Huh?" Becky appeared startled, pushing her mousy brown hair away from her face as she did so.

"Sorry, did not mean to scare you. You seem to be, well... distracted tonight."

"Do I? I'm not, honestly, just a bit, well..."

"Distracted!"

"Not distracted, sleepy."

"You work too hard, is why! Beyond even what's expected and required of med school. Or legal requirements!"

Becky rubbed her forehead wearily. Her head was pounding, and she didn't want to get into another fight with Stefano. In fact, she was stiff all over. She could just go for a long hot bath and body rub right now.

Stefano, noticing the look of pain on her face, backed off a bit. Instead of continuing what could have developed into a full-blown fight, he walked around to where she was sitting and, surprising her, he started to give her shoulders a rub. Becky flashed him a small look of gratitude accompanied by a soft groan.

"Come here." He said helping her to her feet. "How about we go find a movie to watch and just relax for a while? I will even throw in a foot rub."

"That sounds good." Becky replied a look of relief flashed across the delicate features of her pale face.

~~~~~~

Becky barely got through the hour of the movie before she fell asleep. The combination of exhaustion, alcohol and the day's events had taken their toll. Stefano decided to leave her there as he watched the action happen on screen. He liked the feel of her body resting against him, her head laid on his chest as they had draped a blanket around them.

It had just seemed so natural to sit like that and she had not protested as he wrapped his arms around her again. In fact, she had seemed content. However, the movie was over, and it was getting late. Glancing at the clock, Stefano inwardly cursed at how late it was, his own shift at the hospital loomed ominously closer.

Looking at the sleeping beauty laid in his arms, he smiled. Now he had the problem of getting her up the stairs. He managed to raise her up into a more secure position and into his arms fairly easily, though the carrying upstairs was much trickier. That safely achieved, he laid her down on her bed and was just pulling the covers over her when she woke up.

"Stefano?" She asked sleepily.

"Yes Becky?"

"Did I fall asleep?" She questioned, clearly not with the rest of the world.

Stefano found it kind of endearing. He found everything about Becky appealing though. Just a bit too appealing for things to be comfortable in certain areas at times, including now. And the compromising position he found himself in was not helping. If he was not a complete gentleman his eye line would be directly gazing down Becky's V-neck top. Not like he had not taken sneaky glances down there when he thought she would not realise in the past. After all, he was only human. However, he was busy gazing at her face at that moment in time, trying to think about anything but what was truly on his mind.

"Stefano?" She asked again sounding slightly more alert this time. "Yes?" He asked, laying the covers over her as he did.

She seemed hesitant, like she was carefully considering her next words.

"Could you stay with me for a while?"

That was not what Stefano had expected her to say. That was not what she had meant to say either!

"Stay with you?" he asked stalling for time, trying to work out an appropriate response to her request. He pushed a hand through his own curly hair as he also pulled his white teeshirt down over his abdomen, it having dragged up from the effort of carrying her.

"Yes, stay. Please" She whispered. Despite her slip of the tongue, it was obvious that she was going to have to instigate the action, again, if they were going to move their friendship further. She lifted the cotton covers up and motioned for Stefano to slip under them.

"I'm not sure about this." Stefano responded. His eyes darted around the room as he tried to process the situation, he had found himself in.

Becky restrained herself from moaning in frustration. If she had been sensible, she would have thought things through instead of shooting from the hip as it were. However, it seemed like her heart was taking over from her logical side.

"I am." She responded after a long moment. Stefano noting the look on her face decided to compromise and tucked her back in before sitting on top of the covers. It was Becky's disappointed look that then prompted him to ask.

"Becky, what is the matter with you tonight?"

What she said next would change their comfortable, if not confusing, relationship. It all came out in such a rush that Stefano could only make out "Bad day at work", "I'm Hormonal" and "I don't want to be just friends with you!"

Actually, that last bit was clear but that was not what Stefano particularly wanted to hear. It was nice to hear it, of course. He was, in fact, flattered and had been feeling the same way, but he was scared to admit it even to himself.

"Woah calm down Becky. Take a breath and say that again!"

"I said can I not feel a little insecure? I have had a bad day at work. It was lousy, beyond lousy and I don't know if that's something I can deal with. I am missing out on so much. And I don't want to be just good friends with you, I love you, I always have Stefano." It was then she realised what she had said and, embarrassed, she turned away and buried her face in the pillow. To Stefano's shock, he heard a sob coming from her.

It is a cliché to say that men get nervous or panic when faced with a crying female. Stefano was someone who adhered to that thought. However, he simply held her hand, making what he hoped were soothing sounds as she let the pent-up emotions of the day spill out.

After she had cried for a bit, literally onto his shoulder, and he held her and said umpteen words of comfort, she finally settled down. If Becky was following a plan, she would have been more than happy to stray off it the instant he kissed her. It was only a friendly, chaste kiss to her forehead, a simple act of affection. However, Becky saw an opportunity as thought patterns went out the window. She responded with a passionate kiss of her own, pulling him in close and letting her actions express her feelings in that moment. It was finally the need for oxygen that pulled the two apart.

"Whoa..." was Stefano's stunned response. Becky smiled.

"You okay?"

"Yeah." He nodded his head to back up his statement.

"Good. I... kind'a want to do that again."

"Uh huh." Stefano responded, putting a hand on her shoulder. "Don't get me wrong, I really want to as well; it was good. But you have had a lot to drink. I don't want us to do something like that whilst you're in this state."

Becky looked at him confused and then grateful even as she felt more tears starting to form. She pinched her nose trying to regain control of her emotions.

"If you still want to when you've sobered up, then trust me, I am right there with you. And if we are going to lose each other as friends then I want to do it properly. But only if you're really sure." He continued, mentally kicking himself but also confident that it was the right thing to say and do. He briefly imagined his mother nodding in agreement at the choice.

The look on Becky's face indicated that she wanted to do more than kiss that night. If one had to describe it, it was an odd mixture of vulnerability and base desire wanting to escape. If Stefano knew what was really going on with Becky, or if Clara had been around to explain things to him, he would have realised that Becky had been feeling frustrated as of late. It did not help that she had been stressed with both her rotations and the uncertainty that a career in medicine was actually for her. She just needed some form of relief.

But at the same time, even through the haze of alcohol, she also appreciated his care in the situation. She would not be as certain in her actions, and it was true she may regret them, in the cold, sober light of day.

It would be worth the wait though; she had a feeling about that.

~~~~~~

It took a while for her body to recover from the intensity of her tears as Stefano's words had caused another bout. She was vaguely aware of Stefano gently holding her close to him, gently enveloping her against his chest. The smell of the woody tones in his soap lingering around him was comforting to her as she felt the weight of the duvet calm her down further.

"I'm sorry." Becky muttered. "I don't know what came over me."

Stefano smiled softly, wordlessly in response. He continued to hold her close, liking the feeling despite the awkward circumstances. He took a deep breath, breathing in the citrus scent of her shampoo of choice.

"Are we good?" She asked suddenly feeling anxious about her words and actions.

"Yeah." Stefano sleepily responded. "'Course we are. Never apologise for needing to cry it out."

"Thanks. Not what I was referring to though" She replied trying and failing to hide her own yawn again. His words, combined with his comforting actions, felt nice as they took away the last of the tension that was present in her.

"We're good. We are confusing but good." Stefano replied.

"Sleep here tonight" Becky whispered, kissing him on his forehead "Please?"

"Sure. Gee, if getting drunk moves this..." He indicated to the pair of them with a wave of his hand. "Closer to something, we need to do it more often. No matter the circumstances, I like this." He gently squeezed his arms against her to illustrate the point.

"No arguments here. Why did we wait to do that?"

"The Job." Stefano responded as she settled into him. He protectively wrapped his arms around her as he drifted into the land of very sweet dreams.

Becky did not fall asleep as easily as Stefano. She did not want this to be a one night only thing, however if that was what it had to be, at least she could be content with the memory of being held by him. She knew they would need to discuss the status of their already confusing relationship. For now, however, she was content to lie next to him, listening to the soothing sounds of his breathing. To gaze at his peaceful face and enjoy the feel of his embrace. This had been a long time in coming and now it had she was satisfied but wanted more.

And more would happen but that would be a different story.

LOVE STORIES

BY
DENISE SPARROWHAWK

LOVE HEART

He'd said he loved her with all his heart. She'd laughed and told him that a lie was never a good way to start a marriage, that it was not possible to love someone with all of his heart, that there had to be room in there for all the others too. They'd argued. He remembered how cross he'd felt. How he'd accused her, saying she clearly did not love him as much as he loved her.

She had sighed, and told him he was immature, and that one day he would understand. This had not helped but, because he loved her with *all of his heart*, he had swallowed his anger and settled himself into an uneasy truce. His unease lasted nine months, until the day tiny fingers clutched his, and, an unfocussed gaze turned at the sound of his voice.

He looked from his daughter to his wife, and his heart all but burst with love.

REMEDIAL REPAIRS

It had taken a long time; longer than she would ever have imagined. But finally, it was over.

She was free of him. Now her life could begin again.

It felt a little strange, if she was honest, and she didn't quite know how to handle the strangeness. She decided to ignore it and just get on with things. She went out, to the park, to the theatre, to concerts, to art galleries and museums. She met up with old friends and drank tea and ate cake. So much cake! She wondered that there hadn't been a world cake shortage declared. But in the end even the butter cream from a mountain of cake was not enough to plaster over the cracks.

Slowly, slowly the strangeness oozed back into her consciousness.

DIVINE INTERVENTION

Rain thrummed on the roof of the car and streamed across the windscreen. Sooner or later she would have to brave the elements – well, the one element – and face the group gathered inside. Of all the days for a downpour, why today? She would have enough to contend with, she didn't need to arrive looking like a drowned rat too.

She sent up a silent half-hearted prayer to the God she didn't really believe in. She only needed a few minutes break in the weather. Just enough to arrive at the church dry. Perhaps He could send a guardian angel with an umbrella? Ridiculous, she knew. No such thing as guardian angels either. The drumming on the roof of the car eased, then ceased.

Thank heavens! She leapt from the car and made a dash for the church. Behind her, unnoticed, a sodden white feather drifted slowly down the windscreen.

HEARTACHE

Today the still small voice would be heard. She lay quiet, listening to the steady sighing of his breath. Outside the first birds, roused by the gentle lifting of darkness, tested their neighbours' wakefulness. Soon others would wake and add their tentative chirps and chattering to the chorus. And the quiet would be broken. The morning would begin, and she would have to turn her thoughts away from the night and look to the day.

This was not to be an easy day for her, most certainly not for him. He would not understand, and she would not be able to explain. There would be tears and anger and heartbreak. She watched him sleep, the sadness like a stone deep inside her. She could leave now and not face the storm of anguish, but she knew she would not. She would wait for this man - who she loved more than life itself - to wake, and then she would break his heart and hers.

SKIN-DEEP

He felt the first cold, piercing touch of the blade. Pain coursed through him and he steeled himself for the onslaught that he knew was coming. The knife would dig and gouge, clumsily slicing into him, revealing the soft flesh, releasing his lifeblood. Even when they came armed with the sharpest blade, they still lacked the skill that would make the ordeal less painful.

As this most recent assault progressed, he screamed his pain. A silent scream. It would disturb no-one's dream but his own. When it was done, they stepped back and admired their handiwork. He shuddered, and the pain shivered out through his leaves. Sap oozed from the wound as they left, arms entwined, oblivious to the pain they had inflicted. The declaration of their undying love emblazoned in scar tissue on his bark.

"Joe n Suzy 4 Eva"

INK-ON-PAPER

Clutching the book to her breast, she cried. The gathered tears, over-spilling, dangled for a moment in fat droplets at the tips of lashes before dipping to trace a slow glistening trail across her cheek. Heart-breaking sobs broke from the depths of her soul and the tears flowed faster. She dashed them away, her anguish inconsolable.

Words from the book danced through her mind, each sentence remembered, caused a fresh deluge of tears and renewed sobbing. Her chest ached with the effort of breathing, of dragging in the unwanted air to her lungs.

There was no room for breath. Her chest was filled to bursting with the pain in her heart.

She opened the book and stared at a page. A year of words left to her. Beautiful words, meaningful words, words filled with love, with hope. How could he have written so much and yet meant so little? The words mocked her. How naive she had been! How eager to believe. Now she saw them for what they were – false, worthless, empty words; nothing more than ink on paper. She closed the book and coldness seeped into her soul

AUTHOR BIOGRAPHIES

Ange Dunn

Chris Robinson

Denise Sparrowhawk

Ethel Stirman

Irene Styles

Joe Larkin

John Kenny

Kevin Horsley

Micheal Stevenson

Quentin Cope

T.H.

ANGE DUNN

Ange Dunn was born and lives in Hartlepool. She is also known to venture into Darlington where she enjoys playing role games (and oh yeah, seeing her fiancé. That's important too.)

She is best known on the internet as 'pomkeygeek' including Twitter, Instagram and YouTube where she tries to maintain a channel. In a former life she has been a retail assistant, NHS Admin, helped create and run a charity and is now a carer/student/book shop volunteer and Nanowrimo ML.

In her spare time (Ha-Ha) she enjoys reading, writing, musical theatre, politics and pub quizzes.

CHRIS ROBINSON

Chris Robinson was born in Hartlepool, and worked in London, briefly in banking, and then in an antiquarian booksellers.

He continued in general bookselling in Durham and Hartlepool, and then as an English language teacher in London, Middlesbrough and the Middle East before retiring back in Hartlepool.

DENISE SPARROWHAWK
BA(Hons) DipLib.

Denise Sparrowhawk writes flash fiction and very, very short poetry. She is a regular contributor to Paragraph Planet which specialises in 75-word stories. She also has an interest in photography and feels her writing captures moments like a snapshot in words.

Denise enjoys the theatre and contributes to the "Spikemike is breaking a leg..." blog, where she is a regular reviewer. Denise works as a librarian and facilitates the Hartlepool Writers' Group

ETHEL STIRMAN

Ethel Stirman grew up in a coal mining town on the South East coast of Durham. As well as being a mother and grandmother, she has had a varied career from metallurgist to teacher.

Her interests include local heritage, reading, writing and lawn bowls. She belongs to Easington Writers and Hartlepool Writers and has had several short stories and poems published.

Her debut novel "Not a Minute on the Day", the first in a trilogy about life in a coal mining town, was published last year and she is currently working on Part Two 'The Price of Coal'.

IRENE STYLES

Irene Styles is a retired schoolteacher, born and bred in the North East of England. She recently emigrated with her husband to join her family in Canada and is kept busy with her grandchildren on beautiful Bowen Island.

Her new and idyllic surroundings provide inspiration for writing, both poetry and short stories. Irene has had several pieces of her work published in anthologies.

JOE LARKIN

Joe Larkin enjoys writing short stories and has an eclectic approach to his subject matter. His contribution to this anthology consists of a piece of historical fiction and a quasi-philosophical essay, that incorporates a twist of fiction laced with a smidgen of humour.

Joe believes what makes you, you, are your memories and as such remembering, even just the little things, quirky as they may be; the pleasant and serendipitous or life's trials and tribulations, can help stimulate the writing process in general and more specifically. Writing uplifts the human spirit giving worth to the lived experience.

Short stories are a great medium for developing *the hunch* (intuition), to neatly arrive at *the crunch* (crucial point), thus delivering *the punch* (line), "*along the way to your narrative Mandalay!*"

Joe's motto: 'Tentationem gravem esse quam delirans!'

'Try to be more delirious than serious!'

J.K.SNOWBALL

J.K.Snowball, is a writer who is from and lives in the seaside town of Hartlepool.

He discovered writing in his late teens, after developing an increasing love for storytelling.

He loves short stories, a good horror or action film and video games.

KEVIN HORSLEY

Kevin hails from Hartlepool. He has been an amateur writer for over 10 years and a member of Hartlepool Writers Group for around the same length of time.

He mainly writes fantasy fiction, science fiction, horror and poetry though not as frequently as he would like due to a demanding job and family life

An avid reader, whose favourite authors include Stephen King, Clive Barker and Neil Gaiman, to name but a few, is more Wychwood than Badger and likes long walks in the countryside or along the coastline.

MICHEAL STEVENSON

Micheal W Stevenson spent most of his youth daydreaming, discovering a love for crafting new and exciting fantasy worlds. He came to live in Hartlepool ten years ago, a decision that changed his life. He always had an interest in writing but felt held back because of his issues with spelling. After taking a literacy course in 2016, mid 2018, he tried writing once again.

Micheal re-awoke his love for fantasy and with newfound confidence he completed his first rough draft of his first novel. Wishing to learn and improve his skills as a writer, he searched for people who had a similar interest in writing. Micheal joined the Hartlepool Writers Group at the start of 2019, a decision that will change his life once again; a decision he will never regret.

QUENTIN COPE.
MA. MSc.

Having spent a fortunate life engaged in world travel as an aviator, business owner and engineer, Quentin has always felt the only sensible finale for such unbridled adventure is to write about it.

An addicted novelist, he tends to write from experience, characterize people he has truly known and weave story lines around real events of the time.

He considers the narratives he engages in to be ones that matter and Quentin is usually not afraid to approach difficult subjects, especially ones that accurately reflect the reality of life.

Having recently returned from several years in Spain, Quentin has now settled in the North East and can truly call the Hartlepool area his new home.

A prolific writer, Quentin enjoys releasing his work through a mixture of traditional and self publishing channels in the hope of maximizing the benefits of both.

With an extensive presence on social media and the Internet in general, Quentin is fortunate to enjoy the benefits of a broad international readership.

T.H.

T.H. was born brought up, lived and worked in the 'Hartlepools' for most of his life. After semi-retirement from teaching he spent his time struggling with the frustrations of water colour painting alongside the problems of researching local history and the perplexities of 'creative' writing.

~~~~~~~~~~~

THE END

Printed in Poland
by Amazon Fulfillment
Poland Sp. z o.o., Wrocław